BILL HUEBSCH

PROMISE

—— AND ——

HOPE

PASTORAL THEOLOGY
IN THE AGE OF MERCY

Discerning *and* Becoming
a Parish *of* Accompaniment

**TWENTY-THIRD
PUBLICATIONS**
twentythirdpublications.com

NOVALIS

TWENTY-THIRD PUBLICATIONS
One Montauk Avenue, Suite 200 • New London, CT 06320
(860) 437-3012 or (800) 321-0411 • www.twentythirdpublications.com

ISBN: 978-1-62785-498-6

Published in Canada by Novalis

Publishing Office
1 Eglinton Avenue East, Suite 800
Toronto, Ontario, Canada
M4P 3A1
www.novalis.ca
ISBN: 978-2-89688-757-6

Head Office
4475 Frontenac Street
Montréal, Québec, Canada
H2H 2S2

Cataloguing in Publication is available from Library and Archives Canada.
We acknowledge the support of the Government of Canada.

5   4   3   2   1   23   22   21   20   19

 A division of Bayard, Inc.

CONTENTS

Promise and Hope in Pastoral Theology

With the inspiration of St. John XXIII and the guiding hand of St. Paul VI, the Church concluded a pastoral and ecumenical council in 1965. Before the Council even ended, Church leaders began in earnest to implement reforms in order to preach the gospel more effectively in the modern world. The clear calls to *aggiornamento* and *ressourcement* sounded at the Second Vatican Council are continuing to resound in the Church. St. John Paul II's consistent invitation to us to center on Christ and give witness to the self-giving love that he demonstrated on the cross continues to guide us. And Pope

Emeritus Benedict XVI has added strength to that by urging us to cling to the profound and absolute truth of God's love for us, even in an age where absolutes are shunned and people are left to fend for themselves in their search for meaning.

In the second decade of the millennium, Pope Francis awakened within the Church the call to renewal so that, as we move into the third decade, the promise and hope of a renewed pastoral theology stirs the people of God. Building on the work of the Council and post-conciliar developments, the Church has begun to formulate and enact this renewed theology. This pastoral theology is not derived; indeed, it is taking its place as a branch of theology unto itself, not merely the application of doctrine, moral theology, or canon law. It is built on theological principles flowing from the style and approach of Christ and reflecting the continuous tradition of the Church. These principles have provided points of orientation for the pastoral ministry of the Church since the earliest years, even if, for certain periods of our history, we were temporarily disoriented. One of the driving forces behind this theology today is the call of *The Church in the Modern World*, 4, to "scrutinize the signs of the times," both an ecclesial and a Scriptural mandate. This prepares pastoral theology to respond effectively and faithfully to people in the modern world.

Thus, flowing directly from Scripture and the pastoral ministry of the Lord, in continuity with the Church's long history and tradition, and in touch with the needs of modern women and men in today's world, this renewed pastoral theology presents itself. Pope Francis' first apostolic exhortation, *The Joy of the Gospel* (2014), provides insights, dreams, and renewed mission for this theology. Embraced and warmly received by bishops' conferences, the academy, and lay men and women around the world, that exhortation takes its place in the ordinary magisterium of the Church. Pope Francis continued to build on that initial statement with *The Joy of Love* (2016) and *On the Call to Holiness in Today's World* (2018). Drawing on those apostolic exhortations along with the gospels, the Fathers, the continuous teaching of the Church, the work of the Second Vatican Council, and other sources, the current renewal in pastoral theology offers modern men and women the opportunity to be attentive to their consciences and discern what God may be asking of them in their particular, concrete situations.

Pastoral theology is always concerned with persons and their real experiences, and it is shaped by a person, Jesus Christ. Hence, in pastoral theology and ministry, there are points of orientation but no fixed propositions; there are guidelines for operating the parish as a field hospital but no strict rules; there is a methodology for enacting accompaniment, but the only fixed outcomes are its goals: to heal people and restore their hope, to invite and welcome people into the Church in Jesus' name, and to help people become adult Christians of mature faith.

This book is composed of six parts. In the sections that follow, we will treat in some depth each element that comprises pastoral theology and ministry.

In Part One, we will consider seven points of orientation that guide and direct pastoral theology. In short, all pastoral ministry is oriented around Jesus. This will set the stage for our study because, again, pastoral theology is person-centered. The pastoral ministry of Jesus sets us on course for understanding how pastoral ministry should unfold among the people of God today. That ministry is enacted by ministers who are keenly aware of the endless divine mercy that God has offered to them. Pastoral ministry, in short, is enacted by sinners.

In Part Two, we will consider a dozen guidelines for a parish ministry of accompaniment. To begin this more practical section, we will study the theology of availability as understood through the lens of the gospels. We will then turn to the theological idea of mercy as it was practiced by Jesus and taught by the Church throughout its history. In particular, we will study mercy itself as a pastoral guide, how mitigating circumstances in people's lives lead us to treat them with mercy, the principle of putting people ahead of law, and the law of gradualism. We will then turn to practical guidelines for enacting pastoral ministry, including accompaniment and its companion, the art of sacred inquiry. We will consider how the power of darkness can be addressed, the primacy of conscience in pastoral theology, and how we answer the call to holiness.

With those factors in mind, we turn our attention in Part Three to ask about the people who are seeking to be accompanied. We will consider both the "regulars" and the "irregulars" in terms of the status of their primary household relationships. Afterward, we will consider how people discern what God is asking of them in other areas of their lives, apart from those primary household relationships. In this second group, we will consider those seeking help, those who are present but silent, those who are absent, those who are morally self-assured, and those who are religiously self-assured about their spiritual lives.

The primary method for accompaniment is theological reflection, which is our next area of study in Part Four. Theological reflection is proposed as the method for reaching discernment in accompaniment. We will consider what we call "the sources of wisdom," which inform the theological reflection of both the accompanist and the seeker. These sources include Scripture and Church teaching—known together as our Tradition—along with careful scrutiny of the signs of the times. We will survey the various methods for theological reflection put forth over the past several decades before describing the blended method I propose here for use in the enactment of accompaniment. And, since all of this theological reflection and accompaniment activity leads into discernment where decisions are reached, we will consider how we recognize consolation and desolation as factors in discernment well done.

After this, we will change gears in Part Five to study the application of accompaniment in the real world of parish ministry. We will consider *how* people might bring their situations in life to an accompanist and also *what* the accompanist does with that: applying the material garnered from those sources of wisdom: Scripture, Church teaching, and the signs of the times. The goal is to help seekers interpret their experiences based on a carefully honed hermeneutic or "sacred inquiry."

In Part Six, we will conclude our study by considering what it means to put pastoral theology into practice on the parish level. How is it enacted in real parish settings? How does it affect how we celebrate the liturgy, write the homily, celebrate the sacrament of reconciliation, provide faith formation, pastoral care, and ministry to the dying? Here we will also study how a parish prepares for the ministry of accompaniment and trains people to be ready to provide it.

PART ONE

Points of Orientation for Pastoral Theology

Encounter with the person of Jesus Christ

Sinners leading other sinners

A personalist theology

Liturgy as the source and summit

The Paschal Mystery: Self-giving love

God is still speaking

Grace is sufficient

1. ENCOUNTER WITH THE PERSON OF JESUS CHRIST

Our first point of orientation leads to an encounter. Pastoral theology turns and pivots on the presence and grace of Jesus Christ in all we teach and do.

All pastoral theology flows from the life and ministry of Jesus Christ. He is the primordial pastor, the exemplar of accompaniment, and therefore the model for how we envision and articulate pastoral theology. Jesus is not only the model but also the Lord, and we in pastoral theology are invited to give our hearts to him. We are called to act like Jesus when we discuss pastoral theology or enact pastoral ministry on his behalf.

The Kerygma: The core message

The core of our faith is believing that God loves us without end, even when we act selfishly and allow darkness into our lives. In those times of darkness, it is Jesus who guides us back to streams of living water. He forgives our sins and saves us. He is the one, in short, who time and again brings life out of death for us. Jesus invites us to learn the art of self-giving love, to die to ourselves as we love others. In each act of pastoral ministry—whether the homily, a religious ed class, a visit to the sick, a moment of accompaniment, or the sacrament of reconciliation—this good news must be evident to all.

We orient all we do around this reality. In Christ, love is stronger than hate. The light has come into the world, and the darkness cannot overcome it. As we read in *The Joy of the Gospel*, 164: "On the lips of the catechist the first proclamation must ring out over and over: 'Jesus Christ loves you; he gave his life to save you; and now he is living at your side every day to enlighten, strengthen and free you.'"

In *The Joy of the Gospel*, 3, we receive this invitation:

> I invite all Christians, everywhere, at this very moment,
> to a renewed personal encounter with Jesus Christ, or
> at least an openness to letting him encounter them; I
> ask all of you to do this unfailingly each day. No one
> should think that this invitation is not meant for him
> or her....The Lord does not disappoint those who take
> this risk; whenever we take a step towards Jesus, we
> come to realize that he is already there, waiting for us
> with open arms....
>
> Let me say this once more: God never tires of
> forgiving us; we are the ones who tire of seeking his
> mercy. Christ, who told us to forgive one another "sev-
> enty times seven" (Mt 18:22) has given us his example:
> he has forgiven us seventy times seven. Time and time
> again, he bears us on his shoulders.

The word "kerygma" is not a common term. It comes to us
from Greek and describes what you just read: the core message of our faith, the essential good news that we tell people.
Jesus walks with each of us personally in our own lives. He
speaks in the depths of our hearts to each of us. It is our personal sins and selfishness that he forgives. He sends the Spirit
into each of our lives, giving each of us grace to respond to his
offer of love. Only by this grace is such love possible.

This is not something new in our day and age. It echoes the
gospels and what the authors of the pastoral letters had to say.
The Fathers of the Church taught about the kerygma in this
way, as did St. Gregory the Great, the Second Vatican Council,
popes, lay leaders, conferences of bishops, the *Catechism*, the

General Directory for Catechesis, and a host of other church statements and messages from the past two thousand years.

In pastoral ministry, it is Jesus who acts through the ministry of the Church. He and he alone is the Good Shepherd. All pastoral theology flows from the life and ministry of Jesus Christ. Therefore, when we enact pastoral ministry, we do so under the power of grace with Jesus acting through us. He is the power or energy that holds everything together (Colossians 1:15–19).

Our faith is not, first and foremost, in the Church itself. The Church cannot save us. It does not give itself to us in grace. It is an important means and occasion of grace for everyone, but in and of itself, the Church is only a means. It is Jesus Christ in whom we believe and around whom we orient our faith. In an important essay titled "Signposts towards a Pastoral Theology,"[1] Thomas Groome and Robert Imbelli survey the current renewal in pastoral theology. They quote Gustavo Gutiérrez who had declared with splendid simplicity, "I believe in Jesus Christ, not in the theology of liberation."[2]

2. SINNERS LEADING OTHER SINNERS TO MERCY

Our second point of orientation in pastoral theology is that we who enact pastoral ministry are forgiven and loved unconditionally by Jesus. Since we are forgiven, in whose name would we ever withhold mercy from someone else?

We who study and enact pastoral theology are similar to those who come seeking pastoral care from us. Our identity as Christians is oriented around how the self-giving love of Jesus on the cross sets us free. When asked about his own identity,[3] Pope Francis said it quite simply and profoundly: "I am a sinner. This the most accurate definition. It is not a figure of speech, a literary genre. I am a sinner." Stephen Bullivant reported on this for *America* Magazine:[4]

> Our pope's admissions and gestures of humility have, after all, become one of his trademarks....Francis' humility, however, is not like Uriah Heep's: a purely formal show of being "ever so 'umble." Instead, it expresses a central conviction of the Christian faith. As we now know, Cardinal Bergoglio accepted his election to the papacy with the words: "I am a sinner, but I trust in the infinite mercy and patience of our Lord Jesus Christ."

Staying with this thought for a moment, it is essential for every person studying pastoral theology or enacting pastoral ministry to remember his or her own sins. Try to recall your own sins of the past; think back over the decades to some of the really rotten things you've done, the people you've hurt, the selfishness of your own life. Whenever we recall our sins like this, we remember that we have received immense, immeasurable, undeserved, and complete mercy. Remember Psalm 51, which we often pray in our liturgies. Here are the first three verses (italics mine):

> Have mercy on me, O God,
>   according to your *steadfast love*;
> according to your *abundant mercy*
>   blot out my transgressions.
> Wash me thoroughly from my iniquity,
>   and cleanse me from my sin.

> *For I know my transgressions,*
>   *and my sin is ever before me.*

Having our own sins ever before us, as Pope Francis seems to have, prepares us to be pastoral theologians and ministers. It shifts us away from being self-referential. It prevents us from leaping to judge others, from analyzing and classifying them. If we are among the sinners to be saved, we aren't likely to pigeonhole anyone else.

In the story of the woman caught in adultery in John 8, Jesus teaches us about this orientation to our own sinfulness. Here is the text:

> Early in the morning [Jesus] came again to the temple. All the people came to him, and he sat down and began to teach them. The scribes and the Pharisees brought a woman who had been caught in adultery; and making her stand before all of them, they said to him, "Teacher, this woman was caught in the very act of committing adultery. Now in the law, Moses commanded us to stone such women. Now, what do you say?" They said this to test him so that they might have some charge to bring against him. Jesus bent down and wrote with his finger on the ground. When they kept on questioning him, he straightened up and said to them, "Let anyone among you who is without sin be the first to throw a stone at her."

The guideline for pastoral theology embedded in this story is almost too obvious, yet it is one that it is good for us to recall frequently. Jesus has met this woman who, according to the law, was indeed liable for stoning. But Jesus, consistent with all of his ministry, looked into her heart and found there a deep desire, hidden from all but God. He shifted the ground, which leads to our guideline here. He shifted from seeing "a sinner and her encounter with the law" to seeing "a sinner in an encounter with her Lord, that is, with the grace of salvation." He employed forgiveness, mercy, and freedom in his ministry with her.

Section one of the apostolic letter *Mercy and Misery*,[5] in commenting on this pericope, put it this way: "The misery of sin was clothed with the mercy of love. Jesus' only judgment is one filled with mercy and compassion for the condition of this sinner." The gospel text continues:

> And once again he bent down and wrote on the ground. When they heard it, they went away, one by one, beginning with the elders; and Jesus was left alone with the woman standing before him. Jesus straightened up and said to her, "Woman, where are they? Has no one condemned you?" She said, "No one, sir." And Jesus said, "Neither do I condemn you. Go your way, and from now on, do not sin again."

We can see at work here the model of pastoral ministry on which we base what we teach today. Jesus took on the care of this woman as a shepherd would a lost lamb. The encounter with her was personal, unlike the crowd of church insiders who stood ready to stone her. He didn't impose a legal solution on her; he enacted a pastoral solution in her life. His hermeneutic was one of mercy and accompaniment: he asked the key question that set her free. His clear goal was to save her, to integrate her into the community—hence, his call that she should amend her life. He accompanied her with tenderness and had reverence for the action of God in her life. By looking into her heart and calling forth her goodness, Jesus offered this woman a pathway out of sin. He sought and summoned her to new life, expressed in his own non-judgmental, loving posture toward her. "Neither do I condemn you," he said.

What strikes me in this story is the amount of silence the storyteller includes. Jesus twice bent down, writing on the ground silently. The two lengthy periods of silence were purposeful on Jesus' part.[6] I suspect that he wanted to allow the voice of God to echo in the depths of both this woman and her accusers. In that silence, the forgiveness and mercy of God became the resounding message.

This story is reminiscent of other stories from Jesus' life and ministry. One such story is about the woman in Luke 7 who washed Jesus' feet and anointed them with oil. Jesus' answer to the scandalized religious leaders who worried about the presence in the room of this woman, a sinner, was to remind them that this woman was forgiven (verse 47). This is the good news that pastoral theologians always want to announce. It is the kerygma that Pope Francis reminds us to have on our lips first and foremost in every moment of Church life (*The Joy of the Gospel*, 165). We should not judge ourselves any less harshly than we do anyone else. We who are forgiven ourselves no longer hold others' sins against them. Let none of us throw that first stone. We are, after all, sinners leading other sinners to recognize God's forgiveness.

3. PERSONALIST THEOLOGY

Our third point of orientation in pastoral theology is personalist.
The encounter with Jesus is always a person-to-person experience.
Pastoral theology is personalist, flowing from our encounter with the person of Christ. God speaks to each of us, calls each of us to holiness, and attends to each of our sorrows, joys, and hopes. Therefore, the enactment of pastoral theology in a real ministry setting will succeed in a personalist, one-on-one setting.

In Christian personalism, we believe that we should always treat persons with respect and love. We regard the conscience of each person as a privileged meeting place between God and each human. Each person is on a unique journey of faith. For this reason, we do not apply the law of the Church to everyone equally, for example, but we consider each case in light of the individual's conscience.

"I know my own and mine know me" (John 10:14), Jesus reminds us. It was this personalist style of Jesus' ministry that captivated the people of his day. They were entranced by it. The image of the shepherd is a very personal one. As Jesus taught, a good shepherd knows each sheep, each lamb—he recognizes the sound of each one's voice and knows each one's face. Jesus conducted his ministry with this same style and approach. Jesus' ministry was personal, immediate, and intimate. He was radically present to each person who came to him. They encountered the person of Jesus Christ, and he encountered them. It was always person-to-person. He did not shield himself or create a distance between himself and the person seeking his help, nor did he allow law or custom to stand in the way.

Examples of Jesus' personalist style abound. It's difficult to find an example of his ministry that doesn't follow this guideline. In Mark 1, for example, the earliest account of his ministry, he called his disciples one by one. He lifted up Simon's mother-in-law by taking her hand in 1:31, and he responded to a leper in 1:40 also by touching him personally. In Mark 2, he spoke directly and personally to the paralytic who had been lowered through the roof, spoke to Levi one-on-one and had dinner in his house, and claimed the Sabbath as a day for people, not for the law.

He acted in the name of God to offer peace, healing, and comfort. He touched each one, spoke to each one, offered himself to each one. The task of the minister is to enter into the same kind of person-to-person relationship. When people come to us for pastoral help, we do not want them to merely encounter "the Church" as an institution. Instead, we want them to encounter "a person of God" or a member of the people of God. We want them to encounter a real, living, breathing pastoral minister. We who enact pastoral theology now stand in place of Jesus for those seeking our help, and it is our task to help people recognize God's presence and hear God's voice, not to replace God's voice with our own.

All pastoral ministry orients itself around this point. Even when we group people together in the parish as we provide formation, worship, or pastoral care, we must find ways to provide each member of the parish with a personal encounter with us, leading to the encounter with Christ.

4. LITURGY IS THE SOURCE AND SUMMIT

This is our fourth point of orientation. Pastoral theology also turns and pivots on the gathering for, and celebrating of, the Eucharist. Without that, we are nothing.

Our faith is *personal*, but that does not make it private. The way to the heart of the Lord is rarely traveled alone. We are a people of God first and foremost, a family or a community. The heart and soul of our faith journey is the liturgy, where we cannot act alone but must act in concert with our sisters and brothers. The liturgy is a fountain from which flows all we do in pastoral theology and in our Christian lives. It's also the endpoint or goal of what we do. Everything leads us time and again back to the table of the Lord.

This is so vital and important to us that we orient all pastoral theology around it. If you closed down all the parish schools and laid off the staff, if you tore down our buildings and burned all our sacred books, if you carted all Christians off to prison and forbade any talk of faith, we would still be Christian as long as we had the liturgy. But if the schools were full to the doors, if we built shining cathedrals and printed our sacred texts in gold ink, if Christianity became the legal religion of the empire but you took away the liturgy, we would no longer be the family of Christ. The Mass is that important to us. It creates us as the body of Christ. It is the moment when Christ stands among us and is present in the word, the ministry of the Church, the people who gather, and the bread and wine. It's the source and summit of our lives (*The Constitution on the Liturgy*, 10). For this reason, all the faithful are called to full, active, and conscious participation in the liturgy each week (*Liturgy*, 11).

The Constitution on the Sacred Liturgy from Vatican II is a powerhouse of a document. It can be argued that no reform enacted at Vatican II went further to enhance pastoral theology than to have called for "the full, active, and conscious participation of all the faithful" in the Mass (article 11). The overall impact of simplifying the rites and making them more edifying, prayed by the faithful who are to be well disposed, know what they're doing, and taking part (article 14), creates a Church filled with active people ready to roll up their sleeves and get to work in pastoral ministry as well. This Constitution and the one on the Church, more than the Decree on the Apostolate of the Laity, shifted the ground on which lay pastoral ministry is defined.

Furthermore, everything in life—our sins as well as our success in faith—comes with us to the liturgy. At the offertory, we place on the altar our own very selves. And everything in life also comes home with us from Mass. How we live with our family and neighbors, how we raise our children, how we conduct the affairs of our business, how we vote and work for justice are all shaped in the liturgy. Just as the Church would cease to be without it, so we Christians also step away from our source and identity when we step away—or are pushed away—from the liturgy. For this reason, who is welcome at liturgy, who is invited to the table, and who plays what roles: these are all very important questions to pastoral theology. As we read in footnote 351 in *The Joy of Love* and in article 47 of *The Joy of the Gospel*:

> I would also point out that the Eucharist "is not a prize for the perfect, but a powerful medicine and nourishment for the weak."

5. THE PASCHAL MYSTERY

The fifth point of orientation in pastoral theology is that we are each called to live and die as Jesus did. We're called to embrace the Paschal Mystery.

In *The Constitution on the Liturgy* cited just above, the theology of pastoral ministry is described well in article 6, where it says this (inclusive language mine):

> By baptism [we] are plunged into the Paschal Mystery of Christ: [we] die with Him, are buried with Him, and rise with Him; [we] receive the spirit of adoption as [children] "in which we cry: Abba, Father" (Romans 8:15a).

The Constitution here cites the Letter to the Romans, which goes on in 15b-17 to describe how being plunged into the Paschal Mystery prepares us for life in Christ:

> When we cry, "Abba! Father!" it is that very Spirit bearing witness with our spirit that we are children of God, and if children, then heirs, heirs of God and joint heirs with Christ—if, in fact, we suffer with him so that we may also be glorified with him.

Pastoral theology is oriented around this marvelous and incredible reality—that God is like a parent to us, that we are God's own children, that we are even more than that because we are *heirs with Christ* of all that God gives us. Pastoral theology often comes into view in people's lives when they are suffering: bereavement, illness, impending death, loss of love, divorce, alienation, self-awareness, and decisions—all experiences and situations in life that demand our attention. At those times, we have a choice: we can suffer without meaning and lose hope, or we can recognize a call to holiness embedded within the suffering and respond with love.

Pastoral ministry is oriented around helping people hear the divine call embedded in everyday experiences and situations, and that call is nothing less than a call to the same self-giving love that Jesus demonstrated on the cross. In the beautiful words of *Now We Remain*[7] by David Haas,

> We hold the death of the Lord deep in our hearts.
> Living, now we remain with Jesus, the Christ.

6. GOD IS STILL SPEAKING

Our sixth point of orientation is the reality that God stands with us. All that God wishes to reveal to us is fully contained in the life and teaching of Jesus, but what the gospel demands of us is still being revealed day in and day out.

Pastoral theology takes its lead from the fact that God is still speaking to us. It is amazing and remarkable, but God—yes, the creator of the world, Jesus the Lord, and the Holy Spirit— is communicating God's self to each of us and, through discernment, we can hear the voice of God in our lives. Every single day. We orient all pastoral theology and accompaniment around this remarkable reality as we guide people to hear God speaking in their consciences. The question on our minds is always this one: "What is God asking of this person in this particular, concrete situation in his or her life?"

Above all else, the *Constitution on Divine Revelation* restored an important sense of balance to the Church's understanding of how God speaks to us. Faith would no longer be seen as mere intellectual assent to a list of doctrines and practices but as a response to God's self-communication that involves the whole human person. Faith is a covenant that leads to discipleship and Christian living. And this leads to the final point of orientation for pastoral theology, one that is closely related to this one.

7. GRACE

Our seventh point of orientation is the force of grace. Grace is offered without cost to each person, along with the freedom to accept or reject it. Grace empowers or guides us to be all that we're created, forgiven, saved, and loved to become.

The first line of the first chapter of the *Constitution on Divine Revelation* provides us with a dramatic clue about how God speaks to us. God communicates God's own self to us, the document says. In Catholic theology, we call God's self-communication by a name: grace. The entire chapter is devoted to this great truth, summed up in this phrase from article 6, "God chose to show forth and communicate Himself." Here is how chapter 1 opens, in part (italics and inclusive language mine):

> In His goodness and wisdom God chose to reveal Himself and to make known to us the hidden purpose of His will by which through Christ, the Word made flesh, [we] might in the Holy Spirit have access to the Father and come *to share in the divine nature.* Through this revelation, therefore, the invisible God out of the abundance of His love *speaks to [us] as friends* and lives among [us].

Isn't that simply remarkable and almost unbelievable? Theologians have constructed high levels of doctrine and dogma to explain this great mystery. It's easier to believe in a doctrine sometimes than to believe that God is communicating or giving God's own very self to each of us. "What I came to see during the Second Vatican Council," the late Bishop Raymond Lucker[8] once said, "is that revelation involved God's self-communication to us. God communicated the inner mysteries of God to us. And we can never...adequately explain or express the revelation of God."

This powerful experience of God offered to every human being from the moment of conception, this mystery of divine presence, is the basis of all revelation. It is free; the life and death and resurrection of Christ give witness to this. In Jesus, all that God wishes to reveal to us is whole and complete. We await no further word. But as I said above, the truth of what God expects of us is being revealed to us every day in our conscience through listening prayer.

Saint John XXIII's own personal life reflected the conviction that pastoral ministry speaks to all men and women. One day,[9] in speaking with a close confidant, he expressed his grief that so many women and men of good will thought that the Church rejected and condemned them. "But I must be like Christ," he said, referring to the crucifix on this desk. "I open wide my arms to embrace them. I love them, and I am their father. I am always ready to welcome them." Then turning to his guest, he said, "All that the Gospel requires of us has not yet been understood."

TO SUM THIS UP

These seven points of orientation in pastoral theology form the foundation of Christian life and the platform on which we build all our pastoral practices. We (1) orient around the person of Jesus Christ (2) who has forgiven us our many sins and (3) who addresses each one of us personally by name. (4) We meet Jesus in the liturgy of the Church where he stands among us and (5) through which we receive the grace we need to enter into the death of the Lord and so to meet him face to face. (6) God is still speaking to each of us and, (7) through grace, we can discern God's voice in the depths of our souls.

What a treasure this is for us! The light of Christ remains with us, and we remain with Jesus. Pastoral theology is oriented around this and nothing else. As we read in 2 Corinthians 4:7–10:

> But we have this treasure in clay jars, so that it may be made clear that this extraordinary power belongs to God and does not come from us. We are afflicted in every way, but not crushed; perplexed, but not driven to despair; persecuted, but not forsaken; struck down, but not destroyed; always carrying in our body the death of Jesus, so that the life of Jesus may also be made visible in our bodies.

— AN ILLUSTRATION —

John and Mary Ellen

When John called Mary Ellen, the pastoral associate in his parish, to set an appointment for pastoral counseling, she knew something had changed for John. His voice sounded upbeat, and their conversation was full of laughter and hope. She'd been accompanying John periodically since the death of his wife a year earlier. John and Dorothy had been married for thirty-eight years, and her death came after a long struggle with cancer. She was the love of his life, and this loss was devastating for him. Mary Ellen remembered him telling her once that losing Dorothy was like losing an arm in an accident. "I've healed," he told her. "I'm not bleeding anymore. But I know I'll never get my arm back."

John was a regular around the parish, often at daily Mass, and willing to help whenever called. But since Dorothy's death, everyone noticed his abiding sadness and sense of loss. He was working through this in a regular series of chats with Mary Ellen.

Several months after the funeral, one of John's friends convinced him to participate in a weekend retreat. It was a three-day retreat held at a center where participants lodged together for the whole three days. He had never participated in this sort of thing, and John was reluctant about it, but his friend convinced him to do it, so off he went. The weekend consisted of talks, small-group discussions, prayer, liturgy, and meals. To John's way of thinking, they didn't get enough sleep, but when he returned home on Sunday afternoon, it was clear to his children and others near him that something very important had changed.

What had changed? Well, to begin with, when he saw his children after the retreat, he wanted to hug them. John hadn't exactly been the hugging type. He had been a dairy farmer most of his life, and he actually got closer to his cows every day than he did to his own children. But he'd been hugging people all weekend long at the retreat, so hugs it would be, all around, for everyone, even for his sons.

He brought home a Bible, in which he had been underlining phrases and marking them with a yellow highlighter. He had the Bible stuffed full of prayer cards and notes. And he was reading it every day. One of his sons actually asked him one day if he had maybe become Lutheran. To his son, reading the Bible was what Lutherans did. Catholics, he thought, owned Bibles but they never actually read them.

He came home with a deeper love for the Eucharist than he'd ever had in his life. On the retreat, the Eucharist was celebrated in a small-group setting where they were standing near the altar, taking part in ways John had never done before.

But the big change was that he came home happy. Now, mind you, John was never actually unhappy. He was a friendly, well-met fellow, and people would have said he was always happy. But he'd also been dragged by Dorothy's illness through a terrible episode of loss. He was weary of carrying the sadness he felt at losing his partner. He wasn't chronically unhappy, but he had been severely tested.

So now in Mary Ellen's office, John began to tell her about the weekend. Among other things, he mentioned that he was continuing to connect with people from the retreat at local gatherings; he was continuing to read and study. She was

surprised by this; John had been timid about such connec-
tions. Mary Ellen was curious about what brought about this
transformation in John. Like everyone else, she could clearly
see the new lightness of being and a strong sense of hope in
him. So she invited John to tell the story about how this all
happened.

"Well, on the weekend," he began, "someone gave a talk
on..." And then he used two words that Mary Ellen had
never heard coming from this fellow's mouth before—"...on
the *Paschal Mystery*," he said. She was quite surprised to hear
him use that term. Here was "plain old John" discussing the
Paschal Mystery with her like it was a slice of daily bread. John
saw her response but went on. "So, this speaker told us about
how Christ lived and died with self-giving love, but how, really, there is a call embedded in everyday life *for each one of us*
to do that. The speaker told us we would all be called in some
way in our daily lives—maybe quite often—and invited to
give of ourselves and empty ourselves for the sake of someone
else. He said it would be a mystery that we might not understand completely at the time, but that if we do enter into it
and practice self-giving love, lo and behold, we will find there
is a new life to live afterward. We will discover," he said, "that
Jesus is walking with us in friendship, that we can turn our
hearts to him, and that his grace would comfort and console
us." John told her all this in one long, excited sentence. He was
like someone who had just found something new and was
so thrilled to have found it that he just couldn't stop talking
about it and showing it to people.

Mary Ellen told me later that she was speechless in the
face of all this. John continued. "So, after this talk, we were in
our small group; the leader passed a crucifix around the cir-

cle and told us he'd like each of us to tell about a time when we experienced this chance to really die to ourselves. But he said that, if we wanted, we could just hold the cross and not talk, but just think quietly to ourselves. I guess he didn't want to pressure us to talk. Well, I made up my mind then and there that when it came around to me, I'd just do that. I'd just hold it and be quiet. But then people started sharing, and one said this, and another said that, and when it did finally come around to me, I just held that crucifix and looked at Jesus, and then *I don't know what got into me*, but I just started talking. I told them about Dorothy and all that happened with her, and all the sadness and all of it, and I suddenly realized, *that was my call*. I didn't see it at the time, but within her illness was embedded a summons for me: the chance to really love her. I knew right then and there that I'd have a new life after this. I just knew it.

"And then—this is the most remarkable part of it all— when we were at Mass that evening sitting quietly after Communion, *I felt his presence*, Jesus' presence, with me. I heard him tell me that he knew how much I suffered, that he understood about the loneliness of losing Dorothy, and that he was with me in this through these people, through my family, my parish..." and then he looked at Mary Ellen and said, "and even through you, Mary Ellen. Right then and there I realized something so powerful that it brought tears to my eyes. I realized that Dorothy may have died, but before she did, she saved me. She saved me."

A long silence hung in the room. Mary Ellen allowed it to simply be.

"See?" John explained to her finally, "This is the Paschal Mystery. It's not only about Jesus' death; it's about how we have to die. It's not only about him rising. It's about how we rise again from the ashes of our lives. And the thing is," he finished, "the patterns of dying and rising that I establish now in my life are going to be the patterns I take with me when I die. The love in our hearts is all that we take with us into the next life. That's what they told us."

Mary Ellen's evaluation

Mary Ellen reported later that she felt that the tables had turned in their conversation and that John was now accompanying *her*. They talked a while longer and then ended their session, but she was dumbfounded by what had happened. She said later that, quite honestly, she had never experienced the Paschal Mystery as John was describing it.

In terms of the pastoral ministry involved in her work with John up to that point, Mary Ellen was focused on helping John return to functioning well in his daily life. She was concerned about his self-realization based on psychological theory, which she had studied while earning her MAPS degree. But she was startled by this incident and asked later, "Did I help him experience friendship with Jesus, who alone could bring him the healing he sought? Did I help him interpret the events in his life as part of the dying and rising we live through? Did I help him understand the liturgy as a holy moment in life and a point of contact with the risen Lord? What role did transcendence play in our conversations? Was I guiding his soul or offering him a sort of spiritual psychology of self-actualization, all set safely and neatly in the parish offices?"

Mary Ellen may have been hard on herself, but in much of what we do today in pastoral ministry, the transcendent is strangely missing. For some, it seems out-of-date to speak of the power of light and darkness, personal piety and holiness, and our encounter with the Lord. It seems equally out-of-date to speak of eternal life as John did. The renewal taking place today in pastoral theology, however, is giving new wings to the supernatural in the approach to ministry. This isn't to dismiss psychological theory and practice; indeed, they're making a significant contribution to the work of Christ in today's world. But it is to balance that "clinical" dimension with a solid understanding of the transcendent. Jesus is the one who heals and forgives, and religious experience gives depth to all clinical outcomes.

PART TWO

Guidelines for Accompaniment

Offering radical availability

Always acting with mercy

Understanding mitigating circumstances

Putting people before the law

Learning patience and gradualism

Employing a gentle, sacred inquiry

Making restoration and integration happen

Learning the art of accompaniment

Dealing with the power of darkness

Practicing servant ministry

Allowing for the primacy of one's conscience

Answering the call to holiness

We're going to turn to the Scriptures now to try to understand more fully what the pastoral ministry of Jesus was like. We hope to articulate some guidelines that might help us turn our parishes into field hospitals, as Pope Francis invited us to do.[10] When he called the church a "field hospital," the Holy Father was asking us to rethink parish life in radical ways. This means, among other things, to open our doors to all who are wounded or suffering in their lives, regardless of their current "legal" standing in the Church. It means welcoming back all those whom we have pushed away over the years, many of them our own children and neighbors. It means withholding judgment about other people's sins while we tend to their need for healing, comfort, and inclusion. As Blase Cupich[11] put it in an article in *America* Magazine,

> The "field hospital church" is the antithesis of the "self-referential church." It is a term that triggers the imagination, forcing us to rethink our identity, mission and our life together as disciples of Jesus Christ.

As we convert our parishes into field hospitals, the way forward is mapped out for us by Jesus. This is only a map and not a turn-by-turn GPS system. We have to feel and find our way. We know that the first element of our journey will require that we make use of the seven points of orientation we just considered above. These are points outside of ourselves and, as we go, we keep them in our lights.

First and foremost, we must be well-oriented around (1) the person of Jesus Christ and (2) the persons who are most in need of God's mercy. What does it mean to follow the example and model of Jesus as a pastoral minister? What does it mean to have a humble awareness of being sinful and being forgiven? This combined action—following Jesus' example with the humility of a sinner on whom he has looked with mercy—is powerful in pastoral theology and fundamental to understanding how mercy is offered in the concrete reality of people's lives.

It helps to re-encounter Jesus through the lens of his own pastoral activity among the people of his age and, from that encounter, to articulate important guidelines that will govern the rest of the work we do here. The various biblical texts we will treat in this chapter were chosen because of their significance to the pastoral theology and practice of Jesus. They are representative of how the gospels tell the story of the Lord, his work, and his presence.

How we select and interpret Scripture

When we turn to the New Testament to learn about pastoral theology, we do so with our mind and heart open to learn what God wishes to reveal to us in the text. We use a variety of tools to help us interpret the text wisely.

One tool is to avoid what is known as *eisegesis*. Eisegesis is the practice of reading a text or group of texts to prove an already-held point of view or presumption, of "reading into the text" what we want it to say. It stands in contrast to a more objective method for reading the text, which is known as *exegesis*. With the latter, we "pull out of the text" what it reveals. We attempt to discern its discoverable meaning by asking certain questions or making a specific inquiry. Hence, in exegesis, we inquire about the intention and purpose of the author or editor, about the situation of the audience in the first centuries, or about other historical or linguistic factors that may affect its meaning.

Another tool we use to ensure that we are allowing the text to speak to us is to read each biblical story in the context of the entire gospel, rather than lifting material out of its original context to assign meaning to it that may or may not be there. The practice of citing various verses out of context is known as "proof-texting," and it strongly suggests eisegesis.

A third tool we use to help us succeed in understanding the meaning of the text are various reliable Bible commentaries. These commentaries have developed within our community over many centuries and are readily available today. They offer insights and research that would otherwise be impossible for any scholar to obtain on his or her own.

A fourth tool we use is one that's more difficult to name and describe. We avoid what we might call *selective literalism* where we treat one verse of Scripture literally while others figuratively without doing the proper linguistic study. For example, the teaching of Jesus about loving one's enemies. It's a simple and straightforward teaching of the Lord found in the Sermon on the Mount in Matthew 5:44. However, throughout history, church leaders in so-called Christian nations have helped governments interpret this in such a way as to justify viciously attacking one's enemies. Likewise, the teaching of Jesus in Mark 9:47, "And if your eye causes you to stumble, tear it out; it is better for you to enter the kingdom of God with one eye than to have two eyes and to be thrown into hell." We know this teaching is not to be taken literally.

On the other hand, the teaching in Matthew 5:32 regarding divorce and remarriage is treated differently. This text is in the same "sermon" in Matthew as the text cited above about loving enemies. But 5:32[12] is consistently taken in its literal sense, even though the New Testament knew nothing about marriage as a sacramental, covenantal union,[13] or about how the modern annulment process would work. Church leaders have recently reflected on this in two synods dealing with love and marriage. *The Joy of Love* is the exhortation that flowed from those synods. In article 298 of that exhortation, a significant list of mitigating circumstances and exceptions is spelled out. If a Christian marriage is indeed a covenant of self-giving love,[14] then what happens when the bond is broken? When the covenant no longer exists in any form? When love is replaced by alienation, hate, or violence? What is the remaining sacramental nature of that bond?

There is no question that Scripture is the inspired word of God and that it is the normative source of the Christian life and revelation, but as I have said here several times and as St. John XXIII taught, what the gospel demands of us is still being revealed. This revelation is occurring in the consciences of Christians as they discern what God is asking of them in particular, concrete circumstances, including but well beyond questions of marriage and divorce.

For example, for many years, I have been engaged with a project assisting the poor of Guatemala. I recently became aware of a tremendous need in a group of villages near Huehuetenango. I'm asking myself in discernment what I am called to as a Christian regarding my not-overly-large retirement funds. How do I read and interpret the teaching of Jesus to the rich young man in the Gospel of Matthew 19:16–30, the Gospel of Mark 10:17–31, and the Gospel of Luke 18:18–30? Surely, given the condition of so many in the world, I am among the rich. Must I give my possessions to the poor to follow Jesus? Or what about Matthew 25? Can I really plan to say at the final judgment, "Well, I did see you poor and homeless, but I felt I had to protect the security of my retirement fund, so I kept the money instead."

Do you see? How we read and interpret Scripture is very important. We avoid eisegesis, proof-texting, and selective literalism, but we also read the text with an eye to what a disciple is called to do and be. We read it and discern its meaning in the depths of our conscience "where we are alone with God whose voice echoes in our depths."[15]

Jesus is the Source

Bishop Robert McElroy[16] reminds us that the beginning points for our theology—as they were for Jesus' pastoral activity—are the human beings in front of us. We are attentive to the real human suffering, searching, and sinfulness, to the lived experience of the people seeking our care. And how do we approach these people? Always, always with mercy. Today's emerging pastoral theology, Bishop McElroy says, "demands that moral theology proceed from the actual pastoral action of Jesus Christ, which does not first demand a change of life, but begins with an embrace of divine love, proceeds to the action of healing, and only then requires a conversion of action in responsible conscience."

Furthermore, we shall see here as we proceed that this renewed pastoral theology is indeed personalist. It is not satisfied with the idea that, somehow, a law or moral code can be blind to the unique situations and experiences of real human beings. We humans all have our unique limitations, and there are frequently mitigating circumstances at play. People try to follow Jesus the best way they can in light of those limits. We simply cannot apply with equal force a cold and impersonal set of laws to everyone. Each person's situation is unique be-

fore God. Each journey takes its own twists and turns, and
within each conscience, God speaks with us as persons. We
believe that God is pleased with every person who steps forward in faith, even if the step is a small one.

Without oversimplifying this, it is possible to ask in pastoral ministry, "How would Jesus respond to this person, situation, or decision? Based on what we know of his pastoral
ministry, what would be his words or actions toward this person?" By keeping these questions prayerfully before us, we also
keep Jesus at the center of our pastoral activity. What guidelines do we find when we pray with and study the gospels?

1. PRIESTS OR OTHER PASTORAL WORKERS OFFER RADICAL
AVAILABILITY TO PEOPLE SEEKING ACCOMPANIMENT.
Pastoral theology leads to a ministry of availability.

In Luke 19:1–10, we read about a typical encounter between
Jesus and the people of God under his care. It's the story of
Jesus and Zacchaeus. Here's how it begins: "[Jesus] entered
Jericho and was passing through it."

In the first verse of this story, we see embedded a key guideline, one that is repeated in story after story in the gospels.
It is that *Jesus was present* among the people, on the roads
and in the villages, on the lakes and the hillsides, in the synagogues, and even in their very homes. He was not "waiting in
his office" for the doorbell to ring. His ministry was enacted
throughout the region, and it was through his words and actions that people came to believe in the good news.

Such a radical presence and availability among the people
is a key guideline of pastoral theology. We do not sit in our offices either, waiting for people to come to us. Pope Francis has

also named this as a guideline for our renewed pastoral ministry. He asks us to get out of the sanctuaries and "smell like the sheep" (*The Joy of the Gospel*, 24). As Pope Francis taught in article 49 of *The Joy of the Gospel*,

> I prefer a Church which is bruised, hurting, and dirty because it has been out on the streets, rather than a Church which is unhealthy from being confined and from clinging to its own security.

This shifts the context for pastoral ministry from occurring solely at the local church building to occurring in the places where people actually live, and it shifts the nature of pastoral theology from theory to praxis.

In this regard, one might read the text in John 3:16 in this way: God so loved the world that he made his own son radically available to us and empowered him to perform actions that show the love of God in our midst. Available day and night. Available when convenient and when not. Available to saint and sinner alike.

The guideline is that we be available to the people of God and provide pastoral ministry in the places where they live and work, just as Jesus did. This is part of organizing ourselves for accompaniment. And also like Jesus, our availability must be rooted in the values of the gospel: humility, neighborliness, prayer, and a desire to root out selfishness and sin. Notice here—as it is in all the healing stories of Jesus—that Zacchaeus wasn't first invited to come over to the parish church where Jesus could hold a meeting, get his paperwork in order, and determine the next step. This story occurs on Zacchaeus' own turf, which brings us back to Luke 19:

> A man was there named Zacchaeus; he was a chief
> tax collector and was rich. He was trying to see who
> Jesus was, but on account of the crowd, he could not
> because he was short in stature. So, he ran ahead and
> climbed a sycamore tree to see him, because [Jesus]
> was going to pass that way.

And here in the story we see embedded a further insight into the availability guideline we just named. This elaboration resounds in the many stories of Jesus in the gospels. It is that we become available with a warm welcome and a heart full of mercy. And, because we cannot assist or accompany someone who isn't asking for help, it falls to us that we position the parish and the universal Church as places of comfort, safety, and compassion. Availability means making the parish a place to which people want to come. Who would come to your parish seeking help in a difficult situation in his or her life? Only those who trust they will be treated with the kind of compassion and Godly care that Jesus showed to Zacchaeus. So the availability that was such an important aspect of Jesus' life and ministry means for us creating a space in which people will recognize us. We should have a reputation for hanging out with sinners.

This guideline is reflected in Jairus coming to Jesus for help (Matthew 9, Mark 5, and Luke 8). It's reflected again in the woman with the hemorrhage touching the hem of his cloak in the same group of pericopes. It's in Bartimaeus calling out from the roadside in Mark 10. It was that leper who came out of nowhere to find Jesus as he was coming down from the mountain in Matthew 8. Whatever, whoever, and wherever: Jesus was available. It's a thousand people in the anonymous crowds today, crying out for help, starving for healing and good news. Pastoral theology is a theology of availability.

2. MERCY FIRST. *Pastoral theology has mercy at the center of how it is enacted in real people's lives.*

People who want to seek us out may not ask explicitly. Zacchaeus' call for help was demonstrated by him climbing that leafy tree, which showed his desire to see Jesus. We have to be very good listeners to hear people tell us what they want or need in their lives. As with the rich young man who came to Jesus (Matthew 19, Mark 10, and Luke 18) or the woman in Luke 7 who washed and anointed Jesus' feet, the guideline is clear: pastoral ministry unfolds when people ask to know Jesus. This places on us the burden of conducting the work of the Church in such a way that people see us as a place of hope and love. If people see us as a place of judgment and condemnation, they will be unlikely to approach us.

This is a challenge for us in the Church because many leaders feel obliged to "throw the book" at people, especially people whom they judge to be greater sinners than themselves. Pope Francis addressed this in article 308 of *The Joy of Love*:

> I understand those who prefer a more rigorous pastoral care which leaves no room for confusion. But I sincerely believe that Jesus wants a Church attentive to the goodness which the Holy Spirit sows in the midst of human weakness.

And this leads us back to the story:

> When Jesus came to the place, he looked up and said
> to him, "Zacchaeus, hurry and come down; for I must
> stay at your house today." So, he hurried down and was
> happy to welcome him. All who saw it began to grum-
> ble and said, "He has gone to be the guest of one who
> is a sinner."

When Jesus met Zacchaeus in his tree, he knew he was meet-ing someone who was hated for his social sins. Zacchaeus vic-timized others. It's so easy for us to hate sinners! But, as Bishop Robert McElroy[17] points out, "Christ's piercing compassionate embrace, conveyed in the call to eat at the house of this sinner, was sufficient to transform" him and change his life. Our guide-line here is clear, echoing the message of Robert McElroy: in pastoral theology when we are available to the people of God who seek our care, we see with "the eyes of God." This means we learn to see and treat everyone as God sees them: each per-son is a truly precious soul, worthy of our love and devotion, a member of the people of God, and treasured by Christ. There are no sinners who are "better" or "worse" than any others, even if we prefer to think of our own sins as somehow less serious.

Among the chief elements typifying "the simplicity and evangelical power of the Gospel" is mercy. Indeed, as Pope Francis opened the Jubilee of Mercy on December 8, 2015, he placed mercy in the center of the Church. "Jesus Christ is the face of the Father's mercy. These words might well sum up the mystery of the Christian faith," he said. "Mercy has be-come living and visible in Jesus of Nazareth, reaching its cul-mination in him" (*The Face of God's Mercy*, 1).

The Church also places mercy at the center of the *Catechism*, and for that reason we always read the doctrine, canon law, moral codes, and catechisms of the Church with the ears of God. We hear in them the desire of the Church to gently guide all people to God's unending and almost unbelievable mercy. We never lose track of this reality as we accompany others.

Pope Francis is asking us to reflect seriously on how the pastoral ministry of the Church sometimes fails to behave in this way. Who are we to withhold mercy from anyone else? he asks. In whose name do we withhold it? In God's name? Pastoral theology is built in part on this profound spiritual insight.

For Pope Francis, mercy of this sort isn't a mere option in his life; it's a theme. He chose as his motto a phrase inspired by the scene from the Gospel of Matthew chapter 9, where Jesus chooses Matthew, a well-known public sinner, as his disciple. Jesus knew full well what Matthew was like, but he also knew that choosing a great sinner would result in a minister of great mercy. In essence, he said to him, "I know you, but I choose you anyway." The pope's motto is taken from that line: *miserando atque eligendo*. My translation from Latin is "I hold nothing against you, and I choose you." This is what pastoral theology says to the people of the Church. And the people of the Church are waiting to hear this message.

Pope Francis himself in *Misericordiae Vultus*, or *The Face of Mercy*, the papal bull announcing the Jubilee of Mercy, told this story:

> The calling of Matthew is also presented within the
> context of mercy. Passing by the tax collector's booth,
> Jesus looked intently at Matthew. It was a look full of
> mercy that forgave the sins of that man, a sinner and
> a tax collector, whom Jesus chose—against the hesita-

tion of the disciples—to become one of the Twelve. Saint Bede the Venerable, commenting on this Gospel passage, wrote that Jesus looked upon Matthew with merciful love and chose him: *miserando atque eligendo*. This expression impressed me so much that I chose it for my episcopal motto.

3. MITIGATING CIRCUMSTANCES. *Pastoral theology takes into account elements of a person's situation that may reduce or eliminate blame or sin.*

The mercy of which we're speaking here leads us in pastoral theology to pay attention to the mitigating circumstances in people's lives. Paying attention is one of the chief skills in all pastoral theology and accompaniment. Pope Francis has written extensively about mitigation, reflecting a long history in the Church. To mitigate is to make less severe, to reduce or even to remove a penalty from someone. Here's what Pope Francis had to say about it (*The Joy of Love*, 308; italics mine):

> At the same time, from our awareness of the weight of mitigating circumstances—psychological, histori-cal and even biological—it follows that "without de-tracting from the evangelical ideal, *there is a need to accompany with mercy and patience* the eventual stages of personal growth as these progressively appear," *making room for "the Lord's mercy*, which spurs us on to do our best."

Whenever we accompany others in pastoral ministry, we re-member that not everyone is able to make every decision with full freedom. For some, there are conditions in their lives that inhibit or reduce their blame for various actions or situations. The *Catechism of the Catholic Church*, #1735, puts it like this:

> [Blame] and responsibility for an action can be diminished or even nullified by ignorance, inadvertence, duress, fear, habit, inordinate attachments, and other psychological or social factors.

It is essential, therefore, that in accompaniment and pastoral ministry, we consider each person's case carefully. Even if a person appears to be in an objective state of sin, their responsibility or blame for that may be reduced or eliminated, as the *Catechism* teaches. There is a long history in the Church that stands behind this teaching. We never want to suggest that the law is changed or that the ideal is reduced. As Pope Francis put it in article 44 of *The Joy of the Gospel*:

> I want to remind priests that the confessional must not be a torture chamber but rather an encounter with the Lord's mercy which spurs us on to do our best. A small step, in the midst of great human limitations, can be more pleasing to God than a life which appears outwardly in order but moves through the day without confronting great difficulties. Everyone needs to be touched by the comfort and attraction of God's saving love, which is mysteriously at work in each person, above and beyond their faults and failings.

4. PEOPLE COME FIRST. *Theology offers people a pastoral solution to their questions rather than a legal one, even while holding firmly to the teaching of the Church.*

Pastoral theology always puts "people first." First before canon law and first before the machinery of church courts and propositional doctrine. From the early pastoral theologians to Gregory the Great to Pope Francis, the Church earnestly asks that in our pastoral theology the customs, rules, traditions, and even the liturgy of the Church be tailored in each age to communicate the gospel to modern men and women effectively. The welfare and good of people's souls, first and foremost, leads us to be ministers of mercy. Drew Christiansen, SJ,[18] cast this idea in a very clear light recently when he wrote:

> For Pope Francis, *salus populi* is the superscript over his pastoral theology: people, first; the spiritual welfare of people above all. Francis quotes the maxim in *The Joy of Love*, his apostolic exhortation on the family. In context, *salus populi* is Francis' refutation of canonists and moral theologians who put rules ahead of people in a mistaken view of pastoral care.

To the student of pastoral theology, it might seem unnecessary to have to suggest that people should come first. People, after all, are what pastoral ministry is all about: their experiences, journeys of faith, doubts, questions, and situations in life. And yet as Drew Christiansen pointed out, there is a strong temptation among pastors to put canon law or doctrine before people.

But here again, Pope Francis summons the long and continuous tradition of the Church and asks us to embrace it. In an early interview with Anthony Spadaro, SJ,[19] the editor of *La Civiltà Cattolica*, titled "A Big Heart Open to God," Spadaro quotes Francis at length. In his response to a question about his hope for the Church, Pope Francis' first line sets the stage for this movement in pastoral theology (italics mine).

> *How are we treating the people of God?* I dream of a church that is a mother and shepherdess. The Church's ministers must be merciful, take responsibility for the people and accompany them like the good Samaritan, who washes, cleans and raises up his neighbor. This is pure Gospel. God is greater than sin. The structural and organizational reforms are secondary—that is, they come afterward. The first reform must be the attitude.
>
> The ministers of the Gospel must be people who can warm the hearts of the people, who walk through the dark night with them, who know how to dialogue and to descend themselves into their people's night, into the darkness, but without getting lost. The people of God want pastors, not clergy acting like bureaucrats or government officials....
>
> Instead of being just a church that welcomes and receives by keeping the doors open, let us also try to be a church that finds new roads, that is able to step outside itself and go to those who do not attend Mass, to those who have quit or are indifferent. The ones who quit sometimes do it for reasons that, if properly understood and assessed, can lead to a return. But that takes audacity and courage.

In pastoral theology, if you recall, the point of orientation we drew from the example of Jesus was to treat each person individually, offering them mercy and compassion while calling them to reform their lives if needed. The guideline reminds us (and Jesus also knew) that we cannot assist people who are not asking for help. This puts the burden on us as we said above to make sure the parish is a place of comfort, safety, and mercy. We should have a reputation for welcoming sinners and hanging out with outcasts. When people see or hear about us, they should immediately say to themselves, "Oh, those are the people of mercy where I am welcome, no matter what's going on in my life."

"We have learned that God bends down to us (cf. Hos 11:4)," Pope Francis said in *Mercy and Misery*, 16, "so that we may imitate him in bending down to our brothers and sisters." Many people, he said, want to return to the Church. We in parish ministry are the ones who will receive and welcome them. We learn to "bend down" to meet them where they are.

5. GRADUALISM. *Pastoral theology understands that people gradually grow toward the norms and ideals of church teaching.*

The apostles and disciples were Jesus' handpicked team. They traveled with him, learned from him, and were the ones to whom Jesus' revelation was given. But they were certainly slow to get it. In pastoral theology, we always remember this. In Mark 8, for example, Jesus is trying to teach them about the bad influence of the religious leaders of the day. "Watch out," he tells them, "beware of the yeast of the Pharisees" (15). But his disciples got it all wrong. They thought he was talking about lunch. "Then he said to them, 'Do you not yet understand?'" (21).

The failure to understand the powerful mysteries of Jesus is really part of being human. If Jesus' own chosen team was having trouble understanding and following him, why do we expect our sisters and brothers today to follow immediately and perfectly? Peter, above all, was weak. Up to the end, he didn't have the courage and faith to own up to being a follower of Jesus.

And even in the twelve, there emerged an early form of clericalism, of the desire to be treated better than others. In Mark 9, they arrived in Capernaum after being on the road for a while. Here's the text in 33–34:

> Then they came to Capernaum; and when he was in the house, he asked them, "What were you arguing about on the way?" But they were silent, for on the way they had argued with one another who was the greatest.

Really? Jesus had been slowly revealing to them that it was necessary for him to embrace betrayal and death. They also did not understand that, of course (9:32), but to move from the dramatic and powerful teaching on what it means to die to ourselves and enter into the death of the Lord to a conversation about lording it over others shows that they were slow to adopt his teachings.

A key element or strategy in enacting a pastoral theology of mercy is gradualism.

Gradualism, as St. John Paul II taught so clearly,[20] is the long-taught idea that people grow into intimacy with Christ and become able to follow the way of the Church gradually. This certainly doesn't mean that we are reducing the demand of the gospel or changing the law. Few people can perfect their lives in a single step. This is a matter of common sense as well as the teaching of the Church. It's also a matter of grace; we move toward complete charity and perfection only with the grace of Christ. Who could otherwise become holy? It is better to look for the good that people can do within their limits even if it does not measure up to the ideals of the Church than to condemn them whole cloth.

> But I sincerely believe that Jesus wants a Church attentive to the goodness which the Holy Spirit sows in the midst of human weakness, a Mother who, while clearly expressing her objective teaching, "always does what good she can, even if in the process, her shoes get soiled by the mud of the street." *THE JOY OF LOVE*, 308

Hence, we grow able to know, love, and do moral good gradually. Little by little as we mature in faith, we become more able to carry out the demands and expectations of the law. Pastoral theology takes this into account. "For the law is itself a gift of God which points out the way" and this gift is given to everyone. We can follow the law only with the help of grace. As we embrace God's love and endless forgiveness, we become gradually more able to allow this love to transform our lives (*The Joy of Love*, 295).

6. A HERMENEUTICAL ACTIVITY. *Pastoral theology employs the art of sacred inquiry as it helps people discern what God is asking of them.*

Inasmuch as the enactment of this renewed pastoral theology requires that ministers or accompanists help seekers to "read" and "interpret" both the signs of the times and their own experiences and situations in light of the gospel and the teaching of the Church, pastoral theology is a hermeneutical activity.[21] The contribution pastoral theology makes to other branches of theological inquiry is related to an ambiguity that results from the application of this hermeneutic.[22] Spiritual matters are grounded in concrete situations in people's lives, and one does not always clearly perceive the mystery of God's great purpose. Hence, when there is deep sadness or loss, when life seems to lose its meaning, when one feels the sting of moral judgment, or when one is cast outside the flock, pastoral theology and ministry step in to help plumb the depths of God's mysterious ways and interpret the experience. In these sacred moments of discernment, pastoral ministers can help a seeker read and interpret their experience through accompaniment, mercy, and healing.

How an accompanist helps a seeker interpret an experience or situation relies on the learned ability of sacred inquiry. The accompanist gently nudges or leads the seeker into deeper awareness by examining the experience with a specific set of questions. A hermeneutic is just that: a method of interpreting a text or reading a person's experience. Normally, the term is reserved for use in interpreting biblical, wisdom, or legal texts. But it also applies when one is accompanying someone to "read" their lived experience and understand it in light of their faith.

Later in this text, we will spell out what the hermeneutic of accompaniment—or, as we will call it in plainer English, "the sacred inquiry" of accompaniment—looks and sounds like. In the meantime, to understand this more deeply, let's consider an illustration. I want you to meet Clare and Dave.

Clare belongs to an urban parish and has been a member there for more than ten years. She's active and well-known around the parish; she and her family attend the 10 AM Mass on Sundays and come to Communion every week. Recently the confirmation coordinator, Dave, put out the call for small-group leaders, and Clare stepped forward. Dave was trained in accompaniment, so he invited each volunteer to a brief introductory chat before the year began. During the chat, he further invited each one to "tell their story of faith." His purpose was to allow the Spirit to work in the storytelling (which we will see later is an essential element in the method of accompaniment) and also to get to know his volunteers a bit more and for them to know him.

In Clare's meeting with Dave, she poured out her story. She had been divorced by an unfaithful husband nearly thirty years earlier and is now remarried. The whole episode was painful and confusing for her. Her first marriage had lasted only three years. There were no children in that time, her husband had left her abruptly, and he refused to participate in any post-marriage counseling or the diocesan annulment process. She and her current husband, Phil (who is also active in the parish), have been married for almost twenty-five years, and they have one son in college and two other children in the religious ed program. She told this story to Dave because she felt that transparency was best, and she wanted to know if any of this was a problem for Dave or the parish as she picked up the work of a volunteer small group leader in the confirmation program.

The questions that Dave brings to Clare to help her interpret her situation in light of the gospel and the Church form his hermeneutic. They form the basis of the "sacred inquiry" that he might make of Clare. What is Dave's primary concern, his primary inquiry into her situation?

[1] **A legal inquiry.** His primary concern could be her legal standing in the Church. This would entail bringing canon law to bear on her situation and making sure she keeps within the bounds of her canonical status in terms of receiving the sacraments, her example to others, and her current marital status, which, objectively, seems to be one of grave sin and public adultery. He could apply the law to her without regard to any possible mitigating circumstances. Most pastoral leaders in this situation would "send her to the pastor" to let him sort this out. A harsh judgment could mean the end of Clare and Phil's participation in the parish, which some ministers would say is better than having an "admitted adulteress" working in the confirmation program.

[2] **A pastoral inquiry.** His primary concern could be to accompany her and attend to her pastoral needs. This would entail asking about her friendship with Jesus and how this situation affects that. He might ask about her call to holiness and especially the call to die to ourselves as we enter into the Paschal Mystery and stand before the Lord's cross. Has she recognized that call to holiness and responded to it? He might inquire about how she has reconciled her situation within her conscience. Has she reached a point of interior peace with God? Does she believe she is living as God wants

her to? Indeed, she most likely is not an adulteress after all, despite her objective situation. How has she reconciled her situation with what she knows to be Church teaching on the matter? In his interview with her, he may or may not ask all of these questions explicitly, but he may listen to hear about these matters as they emerge within her story.

[3] **A dismissive inquiry.** Or his primary concern could be to avoid the matter. This would entail dismissing Clare's story as unimportant to him and his program, of turning a blind eye to what she has shared. He might think to himself that he needs small-group leaders more than he needs her story to interfere with that. He might be ill at ease talking with people about such personal incidents in their lives, and he may not even hear her story clearly because of that. Or he might even dismiss the teaching of the Church, seeking to gain her approval and retain her as a volunteer.

Each of these potential ways of responding to Clare—and other responses are also possible—demonstrates one potential hermeneutic that Dave might have had as he helped her "read" her situation. The primary concerns we bring to pastoral ministry drive how we help people interpret what's happening. Hence, pastoral theology articulates the hermeneutic most suited to the Church's desire to guide—or evangelize—the faithful to know Jesus better and love the Church more. Because of the obvious importance of this hermeneutic or set of questions in accompaniment, we will treat this in more detail later. For now, it's enough to state the guideline as one that flows from the pastoral activity of Jesus.

And Jesus, for this part, had his own hermeneutic or set of questions. With the woman caught in the act of adultery, for example, in John 8, his questions were pastoral (option 2 above) more than legal (option 1) or dismissive (option 3).

His encounter with the woman in John 8 provides us with one set of Jesus' questions, but, in fact, he asked many of them. According to Martin Copenhaver,[23] Jesus asked three hundred and seven questions. He asked a lot more than he answered. His questions are telling; they form his hermeneutic as closely as we can interpret that ourselves. Asking questions, according to Copenhaver, was a major part of how Jesus conducted his ministry. The questions Jesus asks tell us a lot about him. He clearly understood the struggles of life, the sense of being lost, and what it takes to discern well and come to know what God is asking of us.

For example—and we have space to consider only a small fraction of his questions—Jesus asked the crowds in Matthew 5:46–47,

> For if you love those who love you, what reward do you have? Do not even the tax collectors do the same? And if you greet only your brothers and sisters, what more are you doing than others? Do not even the Gentiles do the same?

What is he asking here, and what is he teaching? His questions continue: Why worry? Why are you so afraid? Do you believe I'm able to do this? What did you go out to the desert to see? Who is my mother, and who are my brothers? How many loaves do you have? Can you drink of the cup? And on and on.

In Mark, Luke, and John, the questions continue. What Jesus' questions all have in common is that they lead the hearer to the interior place of the conscience, and there to discern what God is asking of him or her. In Luke 10:36, for example, he asked, "Which of these three, do you think, was a neighbor to the man who fell into the hands of the robbers?" The listener would have to move to his or her conscience to name the neighbor. He led them to this more than he preached it.

Likewise, how we form the questions we ask of those who seek our help in "the art of the sacred inquiry" must guide the seeker to hear and recognize the voice of God in his or her conscience.

7. TO INTEGRATE AND RESTORE PEOPLE TO FULL LIFE IN THE CHURCH. *Pastoral theology has restoration as the final goal for everyone in accompaniment.*
Which brings us to the next guideline—an important and controversial one. This guideline is embedded in the action of Jesus toward Zacchaeus and Matthew, as well as many others. It echoes how the prodigal father responded to his son in Luke 15 when he immediately threw a party to welcome his son to the table. This is the response made to sinners throughout the gospels and especially in the Gospel of Luke. The fact is that Jesus shared a meal with Zacchaeus at his house. The act of sharing this meal, as the grumbling crowds understood, was an act of restoration and integration, and many who saw this unfold did not approve. "How dare he?" they asked. And this attitude of "how dare he?" was often found among the religious leaders of Jesus' day. In Matthew's house, in the house where the woman wept at his feet, and in many other meals,

he was accused of hanging out with sinners and thereby including them in radical ways in the life of the community.

Some in the Church believe that we should enact a legal response to people's situations more than a pastoral one. These people fear that if we replace the law with mercy, the message of Jesus will be lost. In fact, though, doesn't the opposite happen? When we put a law or doctrine between ourselves and someone seeking us out amid hurt and loss, don't we betray the gospel message and act, not like Jesus, but like the Pharisees who criticized him? When we do that, aren't we replacing Jesus' personalist style with an impersonal bureaucratic style? Doesn't this give the Catholic Church a reputation for lacking compassion? Isn't it a scandal to the world that people who are hurting and most in need of our mercy are refused mercy for many years on end?

Jesus is teaching us a profound truth. The guideline here is that when we assist the people of God who seek us out, the healing we offer also leads beyond forgiveness. It leads to *integration*. Just as it did for the penitent thief on the cross next to Jesus in Luke 23, repentance leads to a place for us in paradise:

> And [the thief] said, "Jesus, remember me when you come into your kingdom." And [Jesus] said to him, "Truly, I say to you, today you will be with me in Paradise."

It behooves us to take care not to be like the elder son in Luke 15. When the Father in his generous and loving ways has forgiven our sisters and brothers, who are we to continue to hold their sins against them?

And what would this integration look like? Let's take a look at how Pope Francis addresses this at the end of chapter eight of *The Joy of Love*, 311–312 and a corresponding footnote (given in brackets; italics mine).

> *At times we find it hard to make room for God's unconditional love in our pastoral activity. We put so many conditions on mercy that we empty it of its concrete meaning and real significance.* [Perhaps out of a certain scrupulosity, concealed beneath a zeal for fidelity to the truth, some priests demand of penitents a purpose of amendment so lacking in nuance that it causes mercy to be obscured by the pursuit of supposedly pure justice.]...
> For this reason, we should always consider "inadequate any theological conception which in the end, puts in doubt the omnipotence of God and, especially, his mercy."
> This offers us a framework and a setting which helps us avoid a cold bureaucratic morality in dealing with more sensitive issues. Instead, it sets us in the context of a pastoral discernment filled with merciful love, which is ever ready to understand, forgive, accompany, hope, *and above all integrate.*...That is the mindset which should prevail in the Church and lead us to "open our hearts to those living on the outermost fringes of society."

If the enactment of accompaniment with its theological reflection and discernment reveals that a person is "right with God" in his or her conscience, we in the Church must learn to trust that. As Pope Francis points out in *The Joy of Love*, 303,

"Conscience can...recognize with sincerity and honesty what for now is the most generous response which can be given to God, and come to see with a certain moral security that *it is what God himself is asking* amid the concrete complexity of one's limits, while yet not fully the objective ideal" (italics mine).

In short, we must "make room for God's unconditional love in our pastoral activity." We must not put so many "conditions on mercy that we empty it of its concrete meaning and real significance." Such discernment should occur as a process of accompaniment that will guide the one seeking our help to become aware of their situation before God.

The usual reference when discussing canon 915 is to people who are living in irregular marriage situations that prevent them from receiving the Eucharist. But Canon 915 actually reads,

> Those upon whom the penalty of excommunication or interdict has been imposed or declared, and others who obstinately persist in manifest grave sin, are not to be admitted to holy communion.

What are the manifest grave sins about which we should be watchful today? Does being rich and retaining most of one's wealth in the face of world-wide poverty not constitute such a grave sin in which the rich obstinately persist? In the Gospel of Matthew, fully half of the sayings of Jesus are teachings about the dangers of wealth, while very few address marriage irregularities. What about people who manufacture war material? How about those who consistently and knowingly endanger the environment? Given the prominence of Matthew 25 in the gospel, we know it is a grave sin when we fail to welcome and care for strangers, refugees, and immigrants, or to care for the poor. And yet, national policies in so-called Christian nations are being crafted to do just that. The final lines of this chapter (44–46) of Matthew make it pretty clear:

> "Lord, when was it that we saw you hungry or thirsty or a stranger or naked or sick or in prison, and did not take care of you?" Then he will answer them, "Truly I tell you, just as you did not do it to one of the least of these, you did not do it to me." And these will go away into eternal punishment, but the righteous into eternal life.

Which grave sins are worse than others?

But for a person for whom there is no mortal sin, even in a situation where there appears to be sin from an objective point of view, we cannot refuse him or her the Eucharist. As we learn in *The Joy of Love*, 301 (italics mine):

> For an adequate understanding of the possibility and need of special discernment in certain "irregular" situations, one thing must always be taken into account, lest anyone think that the demands of the Gospel are in any way being compromised. The Church possesses a solid body of reflection concerning mitigating factors and situations. *Hence it is can no longer simply be said that all those in any "irregular" situation are living in a state of mortal sin and are deprived of sanctifying grace.*

In other words, with well-done discernment in the context of the internal forum or with the help of an accompanist, a person may come to see that the situation in their life conforms to what God is asking of them. There may not be any mortal sin. Canon 915 gets quoted a lot, but canon 912 puts it like this: "Any baptized person not prohibited by law *can and must be admitted to holy communion*" (italics mine). We simply have no choice but to restore the person who has discerned well, to integrate them into the life of the Church, and to joyfully welcome them to the Eucharistic table. In fact, we should remove our shoes in reverence for the powerful presence of God in their lives.

8. AUTHENTIC ACCOMPANIMENT. *Pastoral theology seeks to make an accompanist available to every Christian who seeks one.*
Accompaniment was the strategy that Jesus chose in his encounter with Zacchaeus:

> Zacchaeus stood there and said to the Lord, "Look, half of my possessions, Lord, I will give to the poor; and if I have defrauded anyone of anything, I will pay back four times as much." Then Jesus said to him, "Today salvation has come to this house because he too is a son of Abraham. For the Son of Man came to seek out and to save the lost."

And here we see embedded another guideline for pastoral theology drawn from this and many other gospel stories of healing and restoration. It is the accompaniment guideline. Pope Francis has raised up this feature of the ministry of Jesus as a model for the entire Church. Today we see accompaniment as the primary strategy for pastoral ministry.

Robert McElroy[24] names a three-step process that we learn from Jesus about how to enact pastoral accompaniment. First, we embrace each person without judgment, even if society or church officials judge them harshly. Second, we love them and allow them to tell their story, often in the context of a meal, which is the healing step. Third, we help them discern the voice of the Lord, seeking them out and saving them. This discernment is the key to accompaniment. The goal of all accompaniment, as we have said, is to help the person grow closer to Jesus. In short, the goal is to evangelize the person. And once in the company of Jesus, once the seeker can hear how God is leading them, then reform from sinful or selfish behavior follows.

As Bishop McElroy has pointed out, "Each of these elements of the saving encounter with the Lord is essential. But their order is also essential." We have drawn this from the story of Zacchaeus, but Jesus followed the same guideline with Matthew whom he called from his tax table in Luke 5 or Matthew 9, with the woman caught in adultery in John 8, and with the woman at the well in John 4, among many others. Perhaps the most famous case of accompaniment in the gospels occurs on that road to Emmaus, where Jesus walked patiently with the travelers and gradually revealed himself to them. He did the same with Zacchaeus, Matthew, Martha and Mary, and many others.

Sitting at Matthew's dinner table, Jesus may have broken some societal and religious taboos and laws, but his presence there shows that he looked *beyond* the rule of law to people's hearts. Whereas the religious leaders of the day simply wrote people off because of their objectively sinful situations, Jesus looked past all that and saw their need for healing and love.

He accompanied them, helping them discover the power of grace within their consciences.

Jesus also moved beyond law and custom when he had that long chat with the Samaritan woman at the well. Again, when he forgave a woman whom religious leaders saw as immoral in Luke 7. And again, when he aided the persistent Syrophoenician woman in Mark 7, when he touched lepers in Luke 5, when he healed the sick, and when he went home with Zacchaeus for supper in Luke 19. In all of these cases, he taught us the guidelines and points of orientation that we are articulating here:

- Jesus as the primordial pastor and shepherd;
- Person-to-person encounters of healing;
- Radical availability to people seeking him out;
- Integration into the community symbolized by sharing the table;
- And above all, accompaniment on the journey of faith.

The point is that Jesus, "the Son of Man, came to seek out and to save the lost" (Luke 19:10). He did not let the tradition, the culture, the law, or the disfavor of his critics stop him when he met someone who was struggling in a real, concrete situation. This is a consistent element of Jesus' way of enacting pastoral theology.

What does it mean "to seek out and save the lost?" *Seek out and save*: this is the goal of accompaniment in today's Church. In the first place, it helps greatly if we always have in mind that we need to be sought and saved ourselves. This call isn't merely a call that "we righteous ones" sound for others. Let us join with the tax collector in the temple and pray, "God, be merciful to me, a sinner!"

Second, to be sought out and saved does not mean that one will henceforth live in "absolute perfection." Who but Jesus (or his mother) could do that? We learn gradually how to practice faith within our specific situations in life, even if it is not in complete harmony with the law. To respond when Jesus seeks us out means to listen to the voice of God as it is revealed to us, to know what God may be asking of us in our given circumstances, even if limited by the mitigating factors that often pile up in our lives. To be saved, likewise, is to receive the grace we need to follow the pathway of God as much as we are able, even if not perfectly.

Pope Francis warns us against judging others by standards that are so difficult that mercy is unavailable. To those who wish to demand a complete and perfect reform of one's life before restoration or inclusion in the community is granted, Pope Francis (in *The Joy of Love*, 295) reminds us of the law of gradualism, quoting *The Fellowship of the Family* by St. John Paul II (italics mine):

> For the law…can be followed with the help of grace, even though each human being "*advances gradually* with the progressive integration of the gifts of God and the demands of God's definitive and absolute love in his or her entire personal and social life."

As Jesus' encounter with Zacchaeus was coming to an end, Jesus said something that I think is fascinating and important for pastoral theology. It's a significant clue as to Jesus' purpose and goal in the encounter. Here is the line, quoting Jesus:

> Today salvation has come to this house, because
> [Zacchaeus] too is a son of Abraham. For the Son of
> Man came to seek out and to save the lost.

Jesus calls Zacchaeus a "son of Abraham." There's almost a sense of wonder in his words. He marvels at Zacchaeus' faith, regardless of his sinful past. It's this ability of Jesus to marvel and appreciate what God is doing in the heart and soul of Zacchaeus that is so important for us in pastoral theology.

Remember the person-to-person style of Jesus? It reminds us that it is God who acts in our lives to seek and summon us in many ways. It is God who heals and restores us. It is God who gives us a new heart. Grace is sufficient for us, and when we see the work of grace in the lives of the people of God under our care, our response should be that of Moses at the burning bush when God said to him: "Remove the sandals from your feet, for the place on which you are standing is holy ground" (Exodus 3:5).

It is true that when God speaks in the depths of a believer, this guideline comes into play. We trust and have reverence for the action of God in each person's life. We "remove our sandals" in reverence for the presence of God's grace. Even if we don't fully understand the mystery involved, what God is asking of each person takes precedence over what we might ask of them.

In other words, we do not sit as judges, but we become accompanists: we affirm and include people. It's very difficult to do this. We form judgments about other people's sins very easily. But once we understand that God is acting in that life, we can begin to understand what Pope Francis means in *The Joy of the Gospel*, 169 when he wrote this (italics mine):

> The Church will have to initiate everyone—priests,
> religious and laity—into this "art of accompaniment"
> which teaches us *to remove our sandals before the sacred
> ground of the other.*

Notice once again the three-step process that Jesus followed with Zacchaeus and that was a recognizable pattern in his encounters with others, including his own disciples. These three steps are at the heart of this guideline. First, he embraced the fellow with his whole heart, without judgment, and with positive energy: "Zacchaeus! Come down from that tree. I must have dinner at your house tonight." No further questions asked. A simple, straightforward, and clear invitation.

Second, he allowed Zacchaeus to tell his story, and he listened with reverence. This affirming action may seem difficult to us, especially when we "disagree" with the lifestyle or sins of the person we encounter. But Jesus knew that in the telling of his own story, Zacchaeus would recognize the truth. Jesus offered the same listening ear to those folks on the road to Emmaus in Luke 24, to the woman at the well, to the rich young man, and to many others.

And third, without much difficulty, Zacchaeus discerned that the Lord was seeking him out and saving him. He stood there and said, "Look, Lord, I can do this. I'm giving half my possessions to the poor."

It's no wonder that Jesus marveled at his faith and saw in him a son of Abraham, which is to say, a person of God in every sense of the word. In the story of Jesus and Zacchaeus, Jesus showed himself to be the "master accompanist."

The guidelines we have drawn from this story could have come from many of the gospel stories. Only when he encountered stubborn and resistant religious insiders (see especially Matthew 23) did he give up in exasperation and warn them of the consequences. It took a lot to provoke him to that point.

9. THE POWER OF DARKNESS. *Pastoral theology understands that the power of evil is real and must be constantly addressed with faith and prayer.*
The text we want to consider briefly is in John 13. This is the story of the "last supper" as John tells it. Jesus and his disciples were on their way to the final episodes of Jesus' life and ministry, but Jesus wasn't finished teaching them about pastoral theology. Here are the first two verses of that text:

> Now before the festival of the Passover, Jesus knew that his hour had come to depart from this world and go to the Father. Having loved his own who were in the world, he loved them to the end. The devil had already put it into the heart of Judas son of Simon Iscariot to betray him.

What does this mean? In his apostolic exhortation *Rejoice and Be Glad*, Pope Francis reminds us about the power of darkness and evil. In pastoral theology, this leads us to important guidelines about the supernatural nature of our work. The healing and forgiveness experienced by the people under our care in pastoral ministry come from God alone. Division, selfishness, and hatred in people's lives—understood apart from mental health or other mitigating circumstances—are the work of darkness.

This guideline is all the more important as we increasingly apply mental health solutions to spiritual challenges. The mental health community has indeed contributed a great deal to our understanding of human nature, healing, and recovery, but it cannot replace transcendence and the work of the Holy Spirit. There remains the need to know God and to be aware of the power of darkness in one's life.

In particular, when it comes to the question of evil and deeds of darkness, we read these verses in John's gospel as a warning. Indeed, in our baptismal promises, the Church asks us to "renounce Satan, the author and prince of sin."

I have been praying Compline, the night prayer of the Church, for many years. A certain Bible reading turns up in the cycle quite frequently, often enough that I know it by heart. It's from 1 Peter 5, and it reads:

> Be sober, be watchful. Your adversary, the devil, prowls around like a roaring lion, seeking someone to devour. Resist him, firm in your faith.

"My adversary the devil...?" What does this mean? Even though the authors of Scripture in the first century had limited medical knowledge and tended to ascribe many illnesses to demonic possession (such as leprosy, for example), the early texts of Scripture reveal that the power of darkness remains a real force in our lives and the lives of the people of God under our care in pastoral ministry. Pope Francis points out in *Rejoice and Be Glad* that when Jesus taught his followers to pray in Matthew 6, he taught them to pray that God would "deliver us *from...the evil one*" (italics mine). The evil one to whom Jesus referred in this text is the same one he encountered in the desert in Matthew 4, known as "the tempter" or "the devil."

"Hence," Pope Francis wrote in this exhortation, 161,

> We should not think of the devil as a myth, a representation, a symbol, a figure of speech, or an idea. This mistake would lead us to let down our guard, to grow careless and end up more vulnerable....He poisons us with the venom of hatred, desolation, envy, and vice. When we let down our guard, he takes advantage of it to destroy our lives, our families and our communities. "Like a roaring lion, he prowls around, looking for someone to devour" (1 Peter 5:8).

In practical terms for pastoral theology and ministry, this requires of us that we—leaders and ministers—be in a constant state of discernment about our own work. We must be prayerful, accompanied, and watchful ourselves. A rule of thumb in pastoral theology is that this ministry is something we never do alone. We enact pastoral ministry in the context of the community and nowhere else. We don't become lone actors, believing that we know better than others. We share and consult; we are open and honest with our companions. And we stay watchful.

And what do we watch for? The power of darkness creeps in like a fog, overwhelming us with a sense of desolation. Vinita Hampton Wright has helped me grapple with this. She points out that when we begin to feel that we can't really do that work to which we know (in our right mind and heart) we have been called, the "roaring lion" may be devouring our soul. At these times, we lose confidence in God's ability to guide and support us. "I can't do this," we say to ourselves. "This isn't good enough." We might even say, "God doesn't want this any longer." This is the voice of the evil one.

We know we are in danger when we realize that we've stepped away from turning our heart to Christ, away from praying. We have a growing sense of resentment about the people coming to us seeking help. "Why can't they just figure things out for themselves?" we might ask, or "Why do we have to keep showing mercy to people who clearly don't deserve it?" This resentment might be based in ingratitude on our part. We're simply no longer grateful for the mercy we have received. At Mass, we are dull, unable to pray the prayers that are on our lips. We literally mouth the words without feeling. Or we become selfish about our time, demanding more for ourselves and less for others. We are full of doubt and fear. If my outlook becomes increasingly gloomy and self-obsessed, I am in a state of desolation. I am resisting God or, if not actively resisting, I am being led away from God by other influences.

Another form of desolation comes to us when we start to feel self-assured about what God wants or demands—for us or for the people we are sent to help. If we unilaterally place law, rigidity, or doctrine before mercy as we address people, then we are being driven by desolation, the belief that God cannot be good enough to offer mercy so generously. The idea that God's goodness and love are limited by our own laws is a strong form of desolation in which we replace God's surprising and endless mercy with the limit of our will and, most diabolically of all, we name that as being "God's will."

Jesus recognized this power of darkness in Judas who sat at table with him. He knew that Judas had lost his spirit, his comradery with the group, his faith. Judas allowed himself to fall away from the community and was led to believe that another way was better. He may even have believed somehow that he was doing God's will, that he was helping advance the end mission about which Jesus had told them: that he would have to suffer and die. But in this darkness, Judas lost faith. The devil, like a roaring lion, devoured him, to paraphrase the text in 1 Peter.

The way out of this is precisely what 1 Peter spells out in the lines just previous to the ones we read above:

> Humble yourselves therefore under the mighty hand of God, that in due time he may exalt you. Cast all your anxieties on him, for he cares about you. Be sober, be watchful.

10. THE SERVANT TO THE COMMUNITY. *There are no seats of privilege in pastoral theology.*
The guideline here—which will be illustrated by Jesus' actions at table when he washes the feet of his disciples—is that those who enact pastoral ministry are truly the servants of all. We follow the model of the Lord. All pastoral ministry is an act of service, and pastoral theology never departs from this loving leitmotif. Returning now to this text from John 13, let's continue to unfold the implications for pastoral ministry that we find in it. Again, we read this text in light of the entire New Testament and especially the other three gospels. It goes on to say:

> And during supper, Jesus, knowing that the Father had given all things into his hands and that he had come

from God and was going to God, got up from the table, took off his outer robe, and tied a towel around himself. Then he poured water into a basin and began to wash the disciples' feet and to wipe them with the towel that was tied around him. He came to Simon Peter, who said to him, "Lord, are you going to wash my feet?" Jesus answered, "You do not know now what I am doing, but later, you will understand." Peter said to him, "You will never wash my feet." Jesus answered, "Unless I wash you, you have no share with me." Simon Peter said to him, "Lord, not my feet only but also my hands and my head...."

After he had washed their feet, had put on his robe, and had returned to the table, he said to them, "Do you know what I have done to you? You call me Teacher and Lord—and you are right, for that is what I am. So, if I, your Lord and Teacher, have washed your feet, you also ought to wash one another's feet. For I have set you an example, that you also should do as I have done to you."

In John's story of the last supper, there is no bread and wine. There is only this incredible action of Jesus as he demonstrated both his love for his friends as well as his desire that they, too, would become servants of others. We always read the other three accounts of this supper, in Matthew, Mark, and Luke, in light of this rendering in John.

Jesus accepted his role as Teacher and Lord, but, for him, those roles were not enough. The love he yearned for and wanted to teach his followers was not simply that of a teacher for his or her students. He wanted the kind of love that brothers or sisters have. He wanted deep friendship—which he now offers to us. When we speak of "friendship with Jesus," we aren't referring to what mere acquaintances share. This is a friendship born of self-giving love and self-sacrifice. It's intimate, honest, and built up by frequent conversation.

Every close relationship also needs symbols and actions of love to be real. At this remarkable moment of his life on his way to the cross, Jesus wanted to let his friends know exactly how much he loved them. His dramatic and intimate action eventually helped his friends recognize that his death was an act of love for all of humanity. This action of Jesus underscores "the servant guideline" of pastoral theology as it was stated above, but it is more powerful than that. Jesus is turning "life in the Church" on its head. God himself is the servant of us humans, and, therefore, leaders in the Christian community must also serve the rest. Pastoral ministry isn't in the Church to enforce canon law or punish rule breakers. Its mission is not to make sure that doctrine is always stated in perfect propositions. Pastoral ministry exists in the Church to provide us with a way to follow his suggestion that "you also should do as I have done to you." We should become the servants of all.

One of the customs of the Church seems to violate this guideline, and it's a custom worthy of our attention as we study pastoral ministry, because it symbolizes our true identity. Wherever large crowds gather for a visiting pope, an ordination, oils Mass, or other major event, we celebrate our liturgy because that represents best who we really are as the people of God. I recently watched on television one such occasion when a pope was visiting New York. As the procession entered the church that day, I was honestly startled to see that the cardinals and bishops all marched *in the front of the pro-*

cession, and they were all *seated in the front rows*. The poor and homeless of New York were nowhere to be found. This custom is a remnant of a long period of clerical history that gave privilege and power to the ordained; but shouldn't the poor be seated first? It struck me that day as out of synchronization with the story of Jesus washing feet, which we are considering here. What happened to that bit about the last being first?

Indeed, the bishops should be the ones in aprons pouring the coffee. The homeless, the poor, the marginalized, and the immigrants should have the first seats in the church. How did we turn Jesus' model and explicit teaching upside down? It's not enough to model the washing of the feet on Holy Thursday if we don't follow it the rest of the year.

However, when pastoral workers enact their ministries with humility and reverence in the face of God's actions in people's lives, tremendous healing flows from it. In Mark 10, Jesus is teaching his disciples and all of us about how to succeed in proclaiming the kingdom and leading people to live within it in their everyday lives. It bears repeating again and again as we learn about pastoral theology:

> You know that among the Gentiles those whom they recognize as their rulers lord it over them, and their great ones are tyrants over them. But it is not so among you, but whoever wishes to become great among you must be your servant.

Here Jesus invites all pastoral ministers to an approach that includes humility and service. This pericope reflects the consistent teaching of the Lord regarding ministry. See also, for example, Matthew 18:1–4, Philippians 2:3–4, 1 Peter 5:5–6,

Ephesians 4:1–3, and Micah 6:8. The structures of pastoral ministry, as well as the enactment of our theology, must reflect this teaching of our faith.

Jesus had an opinion on the form of clericalism that puts the ministers in that front row. In Matthew 23, he defines the servant guideline. This is uncomfortable for us to read because our own situation today resembles that of Jesus' time. Here's what he had to say (italics and list format mine):

> Then Jesus said to the crowds and to his disciples, "The scribes and the Pharisees sit on Moses' seat; therefore, do whatever they teach you and follow it; but *do not do as they do, for they do not practice what they teach.*
>
> - They tie up heavy burdens, hard to bear, and lay them on the shoulders of others; but they themselves are unwilling to lift a finger to move them.
> - They do all their deeds to be seen by others; for they make their phylacteries broad and their fringes long.
> - *They love to have the place of honor at banquets and the best seats in the synagogues,*
> - and to be greeted with respect in the marketplaces, and to have people call them rabbi.
>
> But you are not to be called rabbi, for you have one teacher, and you are all students. And call no one your father on earth, for you have one Father—the one in heaven. Nor are you to be called instructors, for you have one instructor, the Messiah. *The greatest among you will be your servant. All who exalt themselves will be humbled, and all who humble themselves will be exalted."*

Jesus' direction to us in pastoral theology could not be clearer, and this pericope reflects the consistent teaching of Jesus throughout the gospels.

11. CONSCIENCE. *Pastoral ministry aims to help people discern the voice of God echoing in the depths of each one's conscience.*
We turn now from Matthew 23 to Luke chapter 6, where Jesus is teaching us about judgmentalism. This text is chosen here because it is representative of Jesus' teachings about the dangers of judging others. (See also, for example, Matthew 7:1–5, John 8:1–8, James 4:11–12, Romans 2:1–3 and 14:1–13.) In pastoral theology, judgmentalism is a danger that undermines the powerful work of God in people's lives. When we judge others and pigeonhole them with labels such as "unchurched," "unfaithful," "living in sin," "disordered," or others, we close off the possibility of grace and shut people down on their journey of faith. In short, we mistrust the activity of God in their individual consciences.

Here is the text from Luke 6:

> Do not judge, and you will not be judged; do not condemn, and you will not be condemned. Forgive, and you will be forgiven.

Here in this verse, which echoes similar material in Mark and Matthew, we hear the clear guideline Bishop Robert McElroy[25] articulated in that 2018 priests' meeting. "The call to change one's life to conform more fully with the gospel is essential to Christian conversion and the achievement of true happiness in this world and the next," he said in that speech. "But that call must be encased in the tender, healing face of a Church which ministers as Christ did, to take root in the present age."

Pope Francis has famously underscored this guideline in his *The Joy of Love*, 305, where he wrote (italics mine):

> For this reason, a pastor cannot feel that it is enough simply to apply moral laws to those living in "irregu-lar" situations as if they were stones to throw at peo-ple's lives. This would bespeak the closed heart of one used to hiding behind the Church's teachings, "*sitting on the chair of Moses and judging at times with superiority and superficiality* difficult cases and wounded families."

The pastoral church is a nonjudgmental church. McElroy calls on us, in fact, to "banish judgmentalism from the life of the Church and replace it with the constantly affirming love of Jesus Christ. And in doing so," he said, "we will be-come the truly inclusive community that the Church, both by its charter and its intrinsic mission, was always called to be." In pastoral theology, this factor is a primary one because, as I said above, the purpose of our pastoral work is evangeli-zation. It is to help people come to know Jesus and love the Church more fully. The discernment needed for that happens within each one's conscience. All belief is interiorized in this way. Mere exterior adherence to doctrine or moral codes is thin and shallow. Hence the danger of judging others based on exterior codes when they may well have found their right place before God.

Our consciences are our deepest inner sanctuaries, where

we find our truest selves. They are that place where God reveals our destiny and purpose. They are the place where Church teaching meets our own human experience in an inner dialogue leading to discernment. Here is where "the signs of the times" play out their influence along with the advice of our accompanists. Here is where God speaks most clearly and distinctly because our conscience is the place where the divine voice defines us. The unique Word each of us is, the single word God wishes to speak to the world through us, is articulated in the conscience of each.

Our conscience is the place where we are, therefore, ultimately, most alone. Not even those we love most—those who see the greatest part of our hidden lives—can know our conscience for us. This is our sanctuary where we go alone to pray. This is where our private prayer and reflection with the liturgy of the Church reveal grace to us. Grace, as I said above, is that force around which we orient all we do in pastoral ministry. It is loving energy that comes from God—indeed, it is God revealing God's own self to us—making it possible for us to become all we're created to be. Grace is realized and accepted in the conscience, in the willingness to let be what the divine force desires for us.

In pastoral ministry, we continually meet people seeking us out to help them make a decision, interpret events in life, or find peace in their particular circumstance or experience. When we are forming our conscience, the teaching of the Church stands next to other sources of wisdom and plays an essential role. Rather than dominating the conscience-forming process, Church teaching helps to guide and ground it. Church teaching, after all, is the collected wisdom of the community. It is our shared "lessons-already-learned."

At times we will find ourselves in tension with Church teaching. At those times, we are bound to follow our conscience. As the *Catechism* says in article 1782 (inclusive language mine): "[We have] the right to act in conscience and in freedom so as personally to make moral decisions. [We] must not be forced to act contrary to [our] conscience. Nor must [we] be prevented from acting according to [our] conscience, especially in religious matters." And here the *Catechism* is quoting *Dignitatis Humanae*, the Second Vatican Council's *Declaration on Religious Freedom*.

But whenever we reach a point at which we discern that we will depart from Church teaching, we are also bound to evaluate our conscience conclusions carefully, speaking with an accompanist, confessor, friend, or pastor. We never take lightly a departure from the norm of the community, for we are inclined at times to darkness as well as to light, as we saw in the power of darkness guideline above. These Church teachings develop over time. They represent wisdom that comes from God alone, directing and forming us for life in these days. Church teaching also emerges from sacred Scripture, constantly new, constantly informing us again of the teachings of Jesus. For the sake of pedagogy, let me repeat that the revelation of God in Scripture does not change, but what the Scriptures demand of us in our time and place—that is still being revealed to us. God is still speaking.

In pastoral theology, we note that to "depart" from Church teaching, following one's conscience after careful discernment and consultation with one's confessor or accompanist, is not to "dissent" from that teaching. We must love the teaching of the Church even if, in a particular case, we cannot measure up to its ideals. Also, our decision to depart from Church teaching does not constitute the remaking of the teaching itself; it simply directs us along a different path.

For example, in the text we treated earlier, when a group of folks came along one day, dragging after them a woman who'd broken the rules and asking Jesus to condemn her, how did he respond? He asked them to look into their own lives, to consider their own hearts: "Are you without sin?" he asked. "Are you so able to condemn?" He asked them to look into their own hearts for this answer, but he gave no further lectures about the rules. He wasn't thereby condoning adultery, but he was demonstrating pastoral ministry with mercy and compassion in the foreground. He called this woman to reform her life, but only after he first embraced her with love.

Reading and reflecting on these scriptural stories can lead us to deep insights about our own lives and the decisions we make there. As article 1785 of the *Catechism* teaches, "the Word of God is the light for our path." In light of the Paschal Mystery, we ask in our conscience: How am I called to die to myself, to sacrifice myself, for the sake of love? This vocation to die to self is at the core of being fully human.

Recall the last line of article 1776 in the *Catechism* (inclusive language mine): "[Our] conscience is [our] most secret core and [our] sanctuary. There [we are] alone with God whose voice echoes in [our] depths." Here the *Catechism* is quoting verbatim from article 16 of the *Constitution on the Church in the Modern World*. The voice that echoes in our depths is God's voice. We can learn to hear that voice and distinguish it from other voices in our culture, society, or busy minds.

Again, *Catechism* article 1785 teaches that we are "aided by the witness or advice of others," and this is the point at which accompanists step in. Our accompanist may be our spouse or a close friend. It may be our parish priest or pastoral minister. These are the trusted ones with whom we walk in community, the ones with whom we may share meals as Jesus did.

We all need such accompanists to help sort through the questions and decisions in our lives. It doesn't matter whether we're priest or teacher or pope, the plain truth is that we do not discern in isolation. Maybe we're people wondering how to possibly make a choice when the options all seem difficult and when sorting or discerning seems impossible. Maybe our marriage has become violent, coercive, abusive, filled with infidelity, or is unholy in other ways. Maybe our sensitivity to the world's poor seems to call us to work for justice. Or maybe we have finally realized how dangerous it is to be wealthy, but we don't know how to change, how to divest ourselves to embrace the gospel more fully.

Maybe we're lonely or angry or hurt or displaced. Maybe we're HIV+ or dying from AIDS or filled with cancer or have Alzheimer's or other diseases. Maybe we're facing life from a childhood that was filled with horror and violence, and we cannot find peace as adults. Maybe we're leaving religious vows or priesthood, or even the Church itself. Maybe we hear only silence when we listen to God and have come to the point where we cannot bear it any longer. Or maybe we're simply slumped into indifference, a dull routine of life that we hate.

Maybe nothing has excited us, aroused us, or stimulated us in many years, but now we want to feel life fully again, and we don't know how. Maybe we've finally come to terms with being gay or lesbian and know our closet doors must open. Maybe we have joined with a life partner or are in a marriage the Church does not condone, and yet we are committed to the ideals of marriage: permanence, fidelity, monogamy, self-giving love, and openness to children. Maybe we're differently abled or suffering from a stroke or have simply lost abilities others consider normal. Maybe a thousand things, a thousand life experiences in which sorting through the intuitions requires a companion.

In pastoral theology, enacted as it is by accompaniment, the conscience plays a significant role. Catherine Clifford[26] provides a salient reflection on this when she points out that the current renewal in pastoral theology "invites us to re-examine the many customs, rules, and disciplinary precepts of the church to ask whether they continue to communicate the gospel effectually." As we have seen here, there is a need to keep the formulation of the Church's rules and precepts up to date; frankly, some may even need a fresh look.

Pastoral theologians follow the principle of moderation articulated by St. Thomas Aquinas. He taught that there "are very few" rules that come directly from Christ. Citing St. Augustine, Thomas taught that the Church should use moderation when insisting on rules, as did the early community in Acts 15, in order "not to burden the lives of the faithful" and make the Catholic faith a sort of slavery. This would be contrary to our long heritage and tradition. For example, in 1 John 5:3, we read, "For the love of God is this, that we obey his commandments. And his commandments are not burdensome."

In pastoral theology and ministry, workers often encounter people for whom the rules have indeed been a burden, one that they are not capable of bearing. They come to us asking for bread—healing and a warm welcome—but we sometimes offer them only a stone: an impersonal formula of law or doctrine that is claimed to accurately reflect the truth of Christ. But what we offer frequently doesn't ring true *in the conscience* of the one seeking our help. Church doctrine remains external to them and doesn't spring from the internal well of grace, where God gives God's own self to us. Our pastoral response to those who do not measure up to our rigid standards is to advise them to align their conscience with what the Church teaches.

Article 41 of *The Joy of the Gospel* addresses this.

> There are times when the faithful, in listening to completely orthodox language, take away something alien to the authentic Gospel of Jesus Christ, because that language is alien to their own way of speaking to and understanding one another. With the holy intent of communicating the truth about God and humanity, we sometimes give them a false god or a human ideal which is not really Christian. In this way, we hold fast to a formulation while failing to convey its substance. This is the greatest danger.

But Catherine Clifford notes, "The most effective teaching, customs, and precepts of the church are not those imposed by an external authority, but rather those that speak to the inner dynamism toward truth and goodness within human persons, who elect freely to set out on this path knowing that it will lead to a fuller and more authentic life." Hence the pastoral solution proposed in theology today is to follow the strategy of accompaniment, to help people discern what God may be asking of them in their concrete circumstance, all formal statements, generalities, and legal propositions aside.

"This effort calls for missionary conversion by everyone in the Church, that is, one that is not content to proclaim a merely theoretical message without connection to people's real problems," according to *The Joy of Love*, 201. And in article 202, we come to understand that accomplishing "this shows the need for 'a more adequate formation...of priests, deacons, men and women religious, catechists and other pastoral workers.' In the replies given to the worldwide consultation [on marriage and family], it became clear that ordained ministers often lack the training needed to deal with the complex problems currently facing families." Indeed, we have our work cut out for us because we have thought for many years that it was enough to stress moral and doctrinal codes without helping people be open to grace. *The Joy of Love* also comments on this in article 37: "We also find it hard to make room for the consciences of the faithful, who very often respond as best they can to the Gospel amid their limitations, and are capable of carrying out their own discernment in complex situations. We have been called to form consciences, not to replace them."

Let's return briefly to the way we began this guideline: Our conscience, the *Catechism* says, is our deepest inner sanctuary where we find our truest selves. It's that place where God reveals our destiny and purpose, our most private self, our divine legacy. Coming to know and believe what God is asking of us in our given circumstance often requires the help of a gentle, tender accompanist.

12. THE CALL TO HOLINESS. *Pastoral theology responds to this call, which is sounded by God within the life of the faithful person.*

If the context for pastoral ministry is the Church, and if the Church is composed of the people of God who are both the enactors and receivers of pastoral ministry, then the hallmark of the people of God and the goal of all pastoral ministry is the journey to holiness. Chapter 5, article 40, of *Lumen Gentium*, the *Dogmatic Constitution on the Church*, describes what this means. In short, holiness means living in the way God created us to live, in the way God forgave and healed us to live, and in the way the Spirit leads us. Discerning that is the work of pastoral theology. Discernment is theological reflection driven by an authentic "inquiry of accompaniment." By this means, all can come to know what God is asking of them in their particular circumstance.

Holiness is thus an interior and lifelong journey of faith shared by all Christians. It is the business of the Church. This isn't new, but no previous council had ever articulated it as we find it in this Constitution. Holiness, as envisioned by the Council, isn't mere obedience expressed as external conformity to moral teachings or a code of conduct. Far beyond that external forum, it implies obedience to the conscience, to the highest impulse of the human spirit. This Council was concerned with the inward journey. Hence the Council fathers wrote in article 42:

> Therefore, all the faithful of Christ are invited to strive for the holiness and perfection of their own proper state. Indeed, they must so strive. Let all then have care

that they guide their own deepest sentiments of soul aright.

This call is universal. This means, for example, that Clare and Phil, the couple who is divorced and remarried without an annulment, *are called to be holy*, and their call comes in the context of their current situation in life. The couple living together without marriage is called. The gay couple is called. The single parent, the non-Catholic spouse, the couple using birth control, the guy who hasn't come to Mass in twenty years, that woman and man who procured an abortion—they are all called. Each priest, each sister, each brother, and each baptized Christian is called. The task of pastoral ministry is to help everyone live in holiness, in daily self-giving, self-emptying love. These people are all beloved of God. He has already forgiven them. They now belong to us and us to them because they belong to Christ. The Church, or in our case here, the local parish, is much more than an enforcer of good behavior and a guardian of orthodox belief; now it also assists everyone, *everyone*, to a life of holiness.

PART THREE

The People of God Seeking to Be Accompanied

DISCERNMENT OF WHAT GOD IS ASKING
IN PRIMARY HOUSEHOLD RELATIONSHIPS

DISCERNMENT OF WHAT GOD IS ASKING
IN OTHER AREAS OF FAITH

Accompaniment, as I said above, is the chief method for enacting pastoral theology. How authentic pastoral accompaniment is enacted is through the regular and consistent use of prayerful theological reflection. This reflection will make use of a well-honed sacred inquiry or hermeneutic of accompaniment.

Within the parish

A first and most obvious form of accompaniment is that
which one Christian offers to another on the journey of faith.
This may happen when a parishioner comes to the parish
seeking help or guidance when interpreting a recent experience or situation such as death, divorce, job loss, estrange-
ment, crisis of faith, aging, illness, conversion, and so forth.
Many leaders in pastoral care and faith formation are already
practicing excellent accompaniment and have been for many
years. Many parish priests employ this as their primary approach to parishioners. Accompaniment is not an innovation
in the Church.

As we add to what is already occurring, we may organize
opportunities for trained accompanists in the parish to meet
others: brief chats for parents of children in faith formation,
invitations for young adults on their way to confirmation or
in marriage prep, visits with children getting ready for first
communion or reconciliation, meetings with families as they
prepare for baptism and then following up after the event,
reaching out to sick or bereaved parishioners, pastoral care
visits, and many other moments of parish life.

We would hope that godparents would accompany the
young couple after baptism, or that confirmation sponsors
would truly accompany the confirmand, but we know that
often this doesn't happen. As we improve how we offer accompaniment in the parish, we may address this. The model is the
RCIA sponsor who walks with and supports the candidate for
baptism or full communion in a much more intentional way.

About certain matters, many people have stopped coming
to the Church for help because we have failed to accompany
them well. Sometimes in the past, we offered mainly a state-

ment of rules or doctrine in the face of a pastoral need. For example, when questions arise among the faithful about matters related to using contraception, cohabitation or civil marriage, gay unions or marriage, ecumenical marriage, a desire to worship in dual traditions, and other matters, people generally knew the Church's response would be predictable and negative. People simply stopped asking, and some of these people are now absent from the parish.

As the Church opens the pastoral door again and allows for the kind of individual accompaniment envisioned in pastoral theology today, the hope is that people with needs of all kinds would step forward to share their journeys of faith and discern what God is asking of them in these various concrete situations.

A note about spiritual direction

Spiritual direction is a form of individual accompaniment, but one that is more formal and regular. One form of spiritual direction, for example, involves a series of regular meetings over months or years, in which there is a mutually agreed schedule, set of goals, and even cost. These meetings might be an hour or two in length, and there might be work between the meetings to which the participants agree.

Another form of spiritual direction occurs in the context of a retreat. Retreats of this kind may last a weekend or for as long as forty days. During such retreats, participants meet with a spiritual director on a somewhat frequent basis—often daily—to follow a series of exercises such as the spiritual exercises of St. Ignatius or *lectio divina*. The kind of accompaniment that occurs within a parish setting is generally not considered formal spiritual direction.

Outside the parish

Accompaniment also happens outside the parish, of course, and is a normal element of many friendships and marriages. It's necessary, however, to distinguish between simply "hanging out" with someone and actually offering them the intentional companionship that accompaniment implies. As accompaniment unfolds in parishes, training people with a method to accompany one another in marriage or friendship will be part of the picture.

To understand how we apply authentic accompaniment in a given pastoral setting in a typical parish, we consider the people of God in a couple of categories.

- **Category 1:** How a person or couple discerns what God is asking of them within their primary household relationship (marriage, divorce, cohabitation, same-sex unions, and others). These are all people who are sorting out how to live in love with others.
- **Category 2:** How a person discerns what God is asking in other areas of life (apart from those primary household relationships). These are people who are sorting out how to integrate faith into daily life more fully.

CATEGORY 1: *Discernment of what God is asking in primary household relationships*

In this category, there are two groups:

- the "regulars"
- the "irregulars"

The regulars are the folks in regular marriages without issues of divorce, remarriage, same-gender relationships, cohabitation, and so forth. They live in regular Catholic situations, and we include in this group those who may be married to a non-Catholic or non-Christian, but for whom no issues exist regarding the canonical legality of their relationship or commitment. These regulars may very well have other burning issues that require accompaniment, but we will return to that in category two.

The irregulars are the ones who live in household or family situations that vary from the teachings of the Church. These are the ones about whom Pope Francis wrote extensively in chapter 8 of *The Joy of Love.* In truth, of course, all the chapters of *The Joy of Love* apply to both the regulars and the irregulars, but he has called out the pastoral care of the latter for special concern. About these irregulars, Pope Francis wrote in articles 296–297 of the exhortation (italics mine):

> "There are two ways of thinking which recur throughout the Church's history: casting off and reinstating. The Church's way, from the time of the Council of Jerusalem, has always, always been the way of Jesus, the way of mercy and reinstatement... The way of the Church is not to condemn anyone forever; it is to pour out the balm of God's mercy on all those who ask for it with a sincere heart...."
>
> Consequently, there is a need "to avoid judgments which do not take into account the complexity of various situations" and "to be attentive, by necessity, to how people experience distress because of their condition." It is a matter of reaching out to everyone, of

needing to help each person find his or her proper way of participating in the ecclesial community....No one can be condemned forever, because that is not the logic of the Gospel! *Here I am not speaking only of the divorced and remarried, but of everyone, in whatever situation they find themselves.*

So that's the agenda for us when we treat category one of accompaniment: the situation in which people live in terms of their primary household and family relationships.

CATEGORY 2: *Discernment of what God is asking in other areas of faith*

In this category, there are five groups:

- the "seekers"
- the "silent"
- the "absent"
- the "morally self-assured"
- the "religiously self-assured"

The seekers. This group includes both regulars and irregulars. How do we accompany people to live more deeply in the mystery of God, trusting in the teaching of Jesus as embodied in the Church? Whether or not their primary relationship at home is "canonically legal," these members of the people of God have needs for accompaniment beyond questions of legality. For example, they have questions and needs related to preparation for the sacraments for their youngsters; they seek assurance about how to faithfully regulate the number of children; they want help to understand illness, growing old, and death; they may have concerns about the preparation for the marriage of their children; they wonder how to forgive others, how to love their enemies, how to live the teachings in Matthew 25, how to welcome strangers and immigrants, and how to respond in a divided political context, and so forth. We call this group the seekers because they sincerely seek to live the gospel more fully but need to be accompanied on that journey. How do we accompany these people?

The silent. We call this group silent because that is often precisely what they are. We see them in the pews on Sundays but rarely at other parish events. They ask for very little and demand nothing from the parish. They rarely attend an adult education event or any other spiritual or educational opportunity. Even though they do not ask for help, God is active in their lives, of course. These benefit from the careful construction of what we will later treat as "the voice of the parish" or, we might say, from the message encoded within the homilies, announcements, invitations, and liturgies of the parish. We must remember that being silent doesn't imply being without faith. Many of these silent ones live lives of generous self-giving and sacrifice, but they keep to themselves. How do we accompany these people?

The absent. In our day and age, this may well be the largest of the five groups we are considering here. These folks are absent for the most part. We may see them on holidays, at weddings, and when there's a funeral. Or we may see them when they have a child to baptize or at first communion time. Or we may often run into them on routine hospital visits. Many of these are absent from Sunday Mass and parish life, but they continue to consider themselves Catholic or ex-Catholic and see themselves as still in the wings of the Church. For many of these absent ones, their faith has also gone cold, and they no longer pray or think much about God. And yet God calls them within their situations "to love and to do good and to avoid evil," as we read in *Catechism* article 1776.

As God does with everyone in every group or category, God continually offers grace to each person. Embedded in their everyday situations—an elderly parent, a sick child, a needy neighbor, the world's poor, the homeless in their city, the desires of their spouses, and many other moments—is the call to die to themselves, and many of these absent and silent ones do respond generously. They may indeed respond more generously than regular Mass-goers! That they're away from Sunday Mass does not mean they're away from God. "Many whom God has," Karl Rahner, SJ, once said, "the Church does not have; and many whom the Church has, God does not have." How do we accompany these people?

The morally self-assured. We call this group self-assured because that's exactly what they are, at least on the surface of their lives. For these people, the need for accompaniment is much deeper. People in this group may have lost their way to the light of Christ but remain self-assured that they're on the right pathway. People in this group have wandered into the areas of darkness in human life: deep and mortal sinfulness from which a return is more difficult but never impossible. They may still be at Mass regularly (possibly even presiding), but at home, in private, they may be enmeshed in pornography, violence, abuse, adultery, hatred, revenge, theft, rape, hoarding money, abortion, murder, prejudice, or the outright rejection of Matthew 25. How do we accompany these people?

We know that we cannot accompany anyone who is not seeking to grow spiritually or who is not asking for help. The morally self-assured rarely ask for such help. They may very well feel that Matthew 25, for example, simply goes too far and asks too much. Or that what happens in their home is "their business" and no one else's, even if it entails neglect, abuse, or violence. Others may deny the reality of sin in their lives, thinking in a self-assured way that they are nearly perfect. How does accompaniment apply in these situations? What is the pastoral plan? How do we reach these members of the family of God?

The religiously self-assured. Another group of the self-assured are those who believe that they—and those with whom they are like-minded—alone have the answers people need. These tend to reach a predetermined judgment about the people of God under our care. They know what is right and what is wrong, and they hold these positions absolutely, regardless of any mitigating circumstances. These self-assured ones believe that, somehow, they have been given the truth by God and that God has now stopped speaking to us humans. No matter how much pain a person or family may be in, the self-assured know that as long as the rules are followed precisely, God will be happy. As we saw above, many times these people replace the generous mercy of God with the strict laws enacted in the Church, and they treat people far more harshly than God would. They do this, of all things, "in God's name."

The religiously self-assured in the Church make poor accompanists because they cannot hear and empathize. They do not even feel they need to listen since they already know the answers and feel very sure of themselves about them. They tend to be pessimists about human nature and particular cases, making them poor companions on the road to healing. We use the term "self-assured" because it is not from God but from themselves that they reach their points of certitude. However, that aside, they feel justified and satisfied with themselves when they can withhold mercy in the name of God.

PART FOUR

Theological Reflection as the Method for Accompaniment

THE NEED FOR THEOLOGICAL REFLECTION

MODELS OF THEOLOGICAL REFLECTION

OUR BLEND: THEOLOGICAL REFLECTION
IN PASTORAL ACCOMPANIMENT

THE NEED FOR THEOLOGICAL REFLECTION

When we say that pastoral theology is an activity rather than a set of propositions or laws, theological reflection is the activity we're talking about. Theological reflection is the principal means through which we help people discern what God is asking of them in the context of accompaniment.

As we have said above, the central concern of pastoral theology is human persons on their shared journey to the heart of the Lord given the boundary of their limits. This journey is characterized by growth, setbacks, desert periods, and leaps into the unknown mystery of God. It is loaded with change as persons grow in age, developing their primary relationships, attitudes, sexuality, financial situations, psychology, and faith. It is also challenged by the social needs of the world around us: conditions such as the fate of the impoverished, the ones at war, immigrants, the care of the environment, racism, greed, pornography, and hate, among others.

Indeed, article 4 of the *Pastoral Constitution on the Church in the Modern World* describes this human condition of change very well. It begins with the famous mandate to scrutinize the signs of the time to interpret them in the light of the gospel. This helps us to understand our world: its explanations, longings, and often-dramatic qualities, the Constitution tells us. Then it lists some of the main features of the modern world as the Council fathers saw them:

- The profound and rapid change in the whole world;
- This change is triggered by our intelligence and creative energy;
- The changes may recoil on us and on our decisions and desires;

- How we think of ourselves and each other also changes;
- This has brought difficulties such as uncertainty about our direction;
- Despite wealth, there is terrible poverty in much of the world;
- There is also widespread illiteracy, disease, and unrest;
- New forms of social and psychological unfreedom are emerging;
- Political disputes of every kind beset nations;
- Opposing camps and conflicting forces are growing more aggressive;
- The peril of atomic war still looms over us;
- We search for a better world but spiritual advancement lags;
- Permanent values seem fleeting now;
- We are torn between hope and anxiety, and we are burdened with uneasiness;
- In short, we search for meaning but can't find it.

Even though written in the mid-1960s, this long list of ills feels almost overwhelming even today. We could, of course, add to the list now more than fifty years later, but how do we cope with this? How do we find meaning? What are the answers to the questions that fill people's souls?

On a more existential level, we might also ask: Who am I? Where am I going? Do life, generosity, forgiveness, or fidelity have meaning for me? What is God asking of me in this concrete situation? How do I hear God's voice in the din of voices from my society and culture? How are the Church and its teachings part of my life? What do I do if my situation or decisions depart from Church teaching?

Into this context of change and questioning steps theological reflection as the means to help us pursue answers to these and other questions. In theological reflection, we step back from the din of life to contemplate quietly all that is in our hearts and souls. We take the question, decision, or experience we are facing and consider it against the backdrop of what we believe about God and the Church. We *reflect* on it, to use the word in its own definition. In this reflection, we open our hearts to the Holy Spirit. We strain to listen and hear the voice of God in our conscience. We also rely on the witness and advice of our companions and accompanists.

Such reflection helps us search deep within the human soul, the conscience, for clues, hints, and signposts leading us forward. Theological reflection is a personal exercise, and yet it also possesses strong communal and ecclesial dimensions. It is systematic, and yet it remains constantly supple and surprising. It is prayerful, and yet it also involves the human intellect as we understand theology and hear what God is saying to us. It is deeply reflective, and yet there is an intentionally studious element within it as we consult the sources of wisdom that inform it.

Theological reflection also takes into account the signs of the times, even when they challenge or differ from Church teaching. It also pays deep respect to human experience and examines that experience in the light of faith. In a sense, our experience becomes our teacher, but it does more than teach. It also provides the forum or context within which we can discern the voice of God as it echoes in the depths of our souls.

As mentioned, in studying or enacting pastoral theology, theological reflection is the central activity in the art of authentic pastoral accompaniment. In reflection of this sort, we approach a question, concern, decision, situation in life, or other matter with a specific method of inquiry. We have a set of questions we ask of ourselves or others to help unpack or interpret the moment and learn from it. We have used the term "hermeneutic" to describe this set of questions.

MODELS OF THEOLOGICAL REFLECTION

There is no need today for us in pastoral theology to reinvent methods for doing theological reflection. Over the past decades, several such methods have been articulated by various theologians. These are used in theological education throughout the Church. They vary somewhat in terms of their approach, usability, and simplicity. They all describe a method for theological reflection known as "contextual theology" because it admits and respects the context of the Scripture, tradition, culture, and experience.

Bernard Lonergan, SJ's method[27] leads the way. In it, he developed a way for theologians to consider the role and result of self-transcendence, moving beyond the self through religious experience into a radical lifestyle of love. He names five stages for reflection: (1) attending, (2) understanding, (3) judging, (4) deciding, and (5) loving. Lonergan's method is helpful in pastoral theology because it opens the door for any Christian to theologize, and it includes an element of discernment, which is essential in accompaniment. The steps outlined by Lonergan are very clear, and his commitment to conversion fits well with the goals of pastoral theology. Lonergan also assumes a deep familiarity with scholastic theology and philosophy, not to mention epistemology, so his method is more useful to professional theologians than to average pastoral ministers.

A second important contributor to methodology is Tom Groome.[28] He suggests a "shared praxis" in which the partners in theological reflection (or catechizing) follow five steps to reach a decision. In this method, participants (1) first share their experience and (2) reflect on it to understand it more fully. (3) Then they consult the tradition and (4) compare their experience with it. (5) Finally, they reach an informed decision. For pastoral theology, this method holds a lot of promise. As with Lonergan's approach, we will borrow from it as we develop a method for our purposes in accompaniment.

John Shea[29] has also contributed to this conversation with an article titled "Theological Assumptions and Ministerial Style." Shea's method (1) honors the essential goodness in every person and their various situations and uses storytelling to surface (2) what God may be asking of each person through their experience. (3) Users move from this point to see themselves empowered for good by grace and (4) transformed by that grace. This requires a skilled accompanist who can discern and identify the presence of God's voice within each person's story, but storytelling is one of the principal elements in accompaniment, and Shea's approach is very valuable to us.

Joe Holland and Peter Henriot, SJ,[30] provide a very practical method in which they spell out a process for reflection that leads to action. (1) The first step is to ask what's happening, to name the experience or situation. It could be a personal experience, the impoverishment of people, the degradation of the environment, or any other issue or experience. In this step, a dialogue exposes how to describe the real situation. (2)

The second step is to ask why. The response to the question of why requires analysis of those who are affected most. It's based on our belief in human dignity. (3) The third step is to dig a bit deeper and ask about the meaning of the experience or situation. What does it mean, for example, that so many people are impoverished while so many others are so wealthy? (4) And the final step is to choose a way to respond to the situation or experience. This method is very practical and is suited to questions of social justice and peace while also contributing to personal pastoral accompaniment.

Stephen Bevans[31] presents an ambitious six models for theological reflection. Each of these models approaches theological reflection from a unique angle. For use in pastoral theology, they offer very helpful insights.

The use of these established models is helpful in theology because they focus our reflection on real issues and problems rather than on theoretical ideas or propositions. They are especially helpful in group settings where pastoral theology is deeply engaged. The challenge in these methods is that analyzing modern experiences, situations, or questions is often quite complex. Too much analysis can swamp the theological reflection and lead only to "desolation"—the feeling that there is no true answer.

Two other methods for theological reflection that are well respected and useful to us in pastoral theology are by James D. and Evelyn Eaton Whitehead,[32] and Patricia O'Connell Killen and John de Beer.[33] In both of these latter models, the method is to consult various "sources of wisdom" that contribute to interpreting the experience or situation. They bring Scripture, tradition, the signs of the times and culture, along with human experience into a sort of grand conversation or dialogue through which a decision is made about how to act or proceed. These two methods are very useful in pastoral theology because they give pride of place to tradition (Scripture plus church teaching), and they follow the mandate of the *Constitution on the Church in the Modern World*, 4 to scrutinize the current culture in which we live.

The Whitehead model follows the steps of (1) attending to the situation, listening to the community and the tradition, and even listening to oneself. They suggest that it helps to suspend any judgment that may form in one's mind before all the facts are "listened to." (2) The second step is to "assert" a pastoral conclusion based on the information at hand. Here some judgments are needed, even if there is conflict. (3) The final stage for the Whiteheads is to reach a decision, and there may be more than one possible way to proceed based on the sources.

Killen and de Beer take a similar approach, (1) first consulting one's experience, (2) followed by becoming aware of one's emotional reaction to that experience. (3) They encourage drawing on images that illustrate and help interpret the experience. (4) Their fourth step is critical. It is to recognize within oneself the slow movement toward insight that emerges as the story is told and held up to the light of the sources. (5) Finally, based on that insight, a decision is reached.

Another element well named by Killen and de Beer takes into account one's "positions." According to them, each person holds certain beliefs, prejudices, attitudes, or opinions. These are our "positions" and they can very much color what we hear and see in the process of theological reflection. For example, here are some positions that one might hold.

The poor are lazy and dirty.

A mother's place is in the home.

Immigrants only cause problems.

The church can't welcome everyone.

They'd still be married if they tried harder.

Only weak people need help.

Gay people are all promiscuous.

God is angry with sinners.

As Killen and de Beer put it in the work cited, "Learning to identify and revise our positions constitutes an important part of growing in faith because our positions can either keep us from seeing God's activity in our lives or make it more obvious to us. Positions have a life of their own."

OUR BLEND: *Theological reflection in pastoral accompaniment*

For purposes of the theological reflection needed for authentic pastoral accompaniment, I propose that we borrow from several of these methods to create a blended approach. I call this approach *The Accompaniment Method of Theological Reflection*. Here is how I describe it:

- We use the Whitehead and Whitehead model to organize the method. Hence, we attend to the seeker's experience, the stories of Jesus, the tradition of the Church, and the culture. In time we invite the seeker to assert a tentative conclusion about his or her situation. And finally, we consider possible pathways on which the seeker can move forward. Together, the accompanist and the seeker consult the sources of

wisdom to reach a decision about that pathway. We
will study these sources of wisdom a bit later, but in
sum they are:

» Scripture and friendship with Jesus,
» Church teaching and tradition,
» The signs of the times and culture.

- In the process, we also make use of the storytelling
  found in John Shea's model. When we invite
  the seeker to tell his or her story, and when the
  accompanist listens without judgment or interference,
  insights and intuitions often open up quite naturally,
  helping the seeker toward a resolution.

- Those insights are often insipient, so in this method,
  we adapt the Killen and de Beer understanding of
  "movement toward insight" to create a process of
  intentional discernment. We invite the seeker to
  identify small steps or insights that help him or her
  reach a point of consolation.

- Because this reflection occurs in the context of
  accompaniment, we also borrow the idea of shared
  praxis from the Groome model. Accompaniment is
  indeed shared. Both the seeker and the accompanist
  must listen for the nudging and gentle prodding
  of God.

- We also borrow the awareness of one's positions
  or prejudices from Killen and de Beer, asking the
  accompanist to be conscious of these as he or she
  proceeds. Prejudices about any element of the
  situation, experience, question, or decision at hand can
  sabotage an open outcome. God is full of surprises.
  Just as God chose Saul, the least likely apostle, so

we find a divine call forward—if we are open to it—embedded in the situations that come to the accompanist.

- As a way of opening up and making use of the sources of wisdom (mentioned above), we also add a well-honed "sacred inquiry" or hermeneutic of accompaniment to our blended method for theological reflection. Such inquiry guides and steers the process to examine carefully how the sources of wisdom inform the seeker's pathway forward.

- And finally, borrowing from Lonergan, we bring to bear a sincere and prayerful element of Ignatian discernment. The underlying question in accompaniment is always the same: What is God asking of the seeker in this particular, concrete situation? What does the seeker hear God saying in the depths of his or her conscience where he or she is alone with God whose voice echoes there? This can be known only through discernment done well.

- Because it is the reality with which we humans live, we also pay attention to the power of darkness as it may play out in this situation. Division, hatred, death, and destruction are not of God. For discernment to yield consolation, it is necessary to attend to any ways in which evil lurks in the discernment.

- Reflecting all the various methods that inform our blended model, the discernment eventually yields a decision, even if tentative and even if it takes much time to reach it. Discernment moves toward decision; it doesn't go on spinning forever. And with discernment well-done comes the question in

theological reflection of how to restore or integrate
this person or couple into the life of the community.

Coming up here, we will study each element of the theological reflection process, but it is not difficult to unfold this in
an accompaniment setting. Laying it out like this tends to
demonstrate and separate each of its several dimensions, but
these elements swim together in actual practice. Here is an
outline of what this looks like in a concrete setting of actual
accompaniment.

- The seeker brings his or her issue to the accompanist.
  We will discuss the setting for this a bit later.
- The accompanist invites the seeker to tell his or
  her story about the experience, situation, question,
  decision, or other matter that is on his or her mind.
- The accompanist listens attentively, clarifying a little
  as needed, withholding judgment, and resisting the
  temptation to interfere or interpret the story at this point.
- At the back of his or her mind, the accompanist pays
  attention to the three main sources of wisdom as they
  may or may not play out in the story:
  » Scripture and the person's friendship with Jesus,
  » The teaching of the Church,
  » The signs of the times and culture interpreted in
    light of the gospel.
- The accompanist also tends to any prejudices or fixed
  beliefs of either the seeker or him- or herself that may
  otherwise hinder or limit the discernment. At the
  same time, the accompanist is mindful of the power of
  darkness as it may play out in this situation.

- Using the art of sacred inquiry, the accompanist may gently nudge the seeker or help the seeker weigh their own personal experience or situation against the sources of wisdom.
- Discernment begins along the way:
  - » The accompanist gains insight from active listening and remains mindful of the presence of Jesus and discerns that to which he or she is called as an accompanist with this person.
  - » The accompanist helps the seeker be attentive to insight from the sacred inquiry, to try to describe that insight, and slowly to discern what God may be asking of him or her in this concrete moment.
  - » Both pay attention to the spiritual force of consolation and desolation.
- The seeker reaches a decision and sketches the pathway forward.
- When appropriate, steps are taken to integrate the seeker into the life of the parish.

PART FIVE

The Person Who Is an Accompanist and the Process of Accompaniment

By way of review, accompaniment is a process that utilizes theological reflection as its principal means. Taken together, these two elements—accompaniment and theological reflection—are the activities that constitute pastoral ministry. Theological reflection includes a process or means of inquiry and interpretation based on a specific goal: helping someone discern what God is asking of them in a given, concrete situation.

Because pastoral ministry is a personalized endeavor, it is not possible for a person without faith to practice or enact pastoral ministry. Therefore, when we describe the theological method in pastoral ministry, we do so from the point of view of the leader or minister involved. There is no such thing as theoretical enactment of pastoral theology. Pastoral ministry unfolds in real time with real people.

STEP 1: BE CLOSE TO JESUS, *a person of the Church,*
a listener, and a person steeped in the art of sacred inquiry
and discernment
This important work is entrusted to the people of God—to all the people of God, laypeople, sisters and brothers, priests and deacons. To become authentic accompanists, certain attributes should be in evidence:

- Live in a close friendship with Jesus. Walk daily with Christ as their guide and helper. Listen to him in prayer. Tell him their own story. Be with Jesus Christ as their Lord and companion. Know Scripture and allow it to sink into their heart.

- Be always conscious of their own sinfulness and need for grace. Keep in mind how often and profoundly they have been forgiven. Let their own experience of receiving mercy drive their desire to give mercy to others.
- Love the Church and its teachings. Know the customs and traditions of the Church. Be at Mass regularly and be in the heart of the parish. Know what the Church teaches and, even if they are not able to live up to its ideals, love and embrace them—and teach them faithfully to others.
- Be a person of their times: steeped in their own culture and aware of the culture of others. Do not be a "prophet of gloom, as though the end of the world is at hand" but believe that God in his wisdom "is leading us to a new order of human relations which, by the very effort of the people of this time, is directed toward the fulfillment of God's great plans for us."[34]
- Be aware of their prejudices and beliefs, especially those that may affect how they judge the seeker. Judgment may be unavoidable, but to keep one's judgments fair one "checks his or her positions at the door."
- Learn how to listen with the heart, how to withhold judgments and offer understanding. Be attentive to the factors that may affect a person's standing: mitigating circumstances, misunderstandings about Church teaching, old information about their situation that may no longer be valid, or small steps leading them gradually in the right direction.

- Learn the art of sacred inquiry, entering into the experience and story of the other with gentle nudges and areas of exploration of ideas and ideals. Accompanists don't merely walk beside the seeker, but little by little they offer them a map to find their way out of the forest.

Parish leaders should not assume that everyone who is baptized, ordained, or in consecrated life is prepared to be an accompanist like this. It is a calling, a vocation. People who have the gift of accompaniment discern it as a ministry. This means that the accompanist both senses this call within his or her soul and is also called by others to enact this ministry. The call to accompaniment often occurs alongside the call to pastoral leadership in other areas such as education, pastoral care, liturgy, or parish leadership roles. But it may also occur much less formally among friends, neighbors, or family members.

As suggested in the outlines above, the accompanist follows several specific steps to prepare and enact accompaniment with someone seeking help.

STEP 2: RADICAL AVAILABILITY

First, accompanists must make themselves available to others in the same way that God made Jesus available to us. Their way of being present should make them appear open and approachable. This means that, in a concrete setting of pastoral ministry, they need to keep hours at times of day or night in which people who need them are also free to approach them. Accompanists develop a reputation in the parish for being people who will not judge seekers as they unfold their stories.

Pastoral ministers cannot accompany anyone who is not asking for guidance. Jesus' healing ministry did not involve him wandering the backroads of Galilee, zapping strangers with his healing touch. When people approached him, he responded and accompanied them to healing and restoration. It's important to note that the people Jesus encountered did not always respond to his word and his touch. The rich young man in Matthew 19 and Mark 10, for example, went away sad because Jesus was asking too much. Jesus often found people of little faith, unable to understand and follow him. At other times, he sat or walked or shared meals with people, accompanying them patiently. Nonetheless, with or without a response of faith, accompanists make themselves available.

STEP 3: TELLING THE STORY

Which leads us to the third step, the actual encounter. Accompanists become like Christ to others, practicing the same level of shepherding he did. In simple terms, they walk with the seekers as they accompany them, just as Jesus walked with those early followers on the road to Emmaus. To accompany is to give ample time, space, and freedom to others so that God can move in their lives. The accompanist is the vessel in which the seekers place their trust. The accompanist allows the seekers to tell their own stories of happiness or pain, gain or loss, belief or doubt, hope or despair. As the seekers become storytellers, accompanists become story-listeners. Pastoral theology teaches that God will reveal himself in their experience. Embedded in their stories—even the most difficult of stories—is a divine call to holiness.

STEP 4: LISTENING TO THE STORY

Accompanists sit with someone who is in need and who has come asking for help. Life is messy and muddled for people sometimes, and folks need help to sort out what's happening to them. People sometimes just need someone to listen to their questions, concerns, experiences, or situations. People seeking such help may ask someone at their parish to listen, but they may more often seek out a friend, a neighbor whom they trust, one of their parents or grandparents, or a co-worker. When they sit down with that person—whoever he or she may be—the seeker merely wants them to listen carefully, without judgment. The seeker wants the listener to hear what they're saying and accompany them as they search for the meaning, purpose, or the pathway forward in which this experience points them.

Pope Francis has asked everyone in the Church to be trained in the art of such accompaniment so that when someone comes to the parish, we can offer them the guiding hand of a pastoral friend. Pastoral accompaniment always has the goal of helping another Christian find his or her way to intimacy with Jesus. Its purpose is evangelization. Therefore, as an accompanist sits with someone and invites them to tell the story of an incident or situation in their lives, the accompanist listens with "the ears of God." Pope Francis described how accompaniment unfolds in *The Joy of the Gospel*, 171:

> We need to practice the art of listening, which is more
> than simply hearing. Listening, in communication, is
> an openness of heart, which makes possible that close-
> ness without which genuine spiritual encounter can-
> not occur. Listening helps us to find the right gesture

and word, which shows that we are more than simply bystanders. Only through such respectful and compassionate listening can we enter on the paths of true growth and awaken a yearning for the Christian ideal.

On the road to Emmaus in Luke 24, Jesus employed this method of inquiry, inviting his co-walkers to tell their story. When they were ready, he helped them connect their story to his own. Their hearts were burning within them, the text tells us, because they recognized the truth in what he said. This truth leads to freedom and happiness. Indeed, whose heart would not be burning?

So, as accompanists sit, walk, or share meals with people seeking help, they follow a similar pathway. As we said above and are repeating here for emphasis, the process modeled by Jesus is to first invite the seeker to tell the accompanist what's happening, what decision they might be facing, what experience they have, or what the situation of their life might be. Because the accompanist knows that God is calling them to holiness and knows that God is active in their life through grace, the accompanist listens without judgment. He or she listens with the ears of God and sees each person with the eyes of God. This person—no matter what their story—is beloved of God.

Active listening allows us to participate in their storytelling. Here and there along the way, when the moment is right for it, the accompanist makes small inquiries about the seeker's understanding of the events they're sharing, their reactions to them, their feelings, hopes, and fears. Accompanists do not accompany for the mere sake of accompanying. Pope Francis writes: "Genuine spiritual accompaniment always begins and flourishes in the context of service to the mission of evangelization" (*The Joy of the Gospel*, 173). Spiritual accompaniment leads "others closer to God…to accompany them would be counterproductive if it became a sort of therapy supporting their self-absorption and ceased to be a pilgrimage with Christ to the Father" (*The Joy of the Gospel*, 170). The accompanist keeps in mind that goal: evangelization. It is a process of helping the seeker to discover Jesus in new and intimate ways, to see the stories of their lives as part of their journey of faith, and to know that they are forgiven, loved, and treated with mercy. Hence, the method of sacred inquiry used by the accompanist is very important.

STEP 5: THE ART OF SACRED INQUIRY

The theological reflection, which is the activity or enactment of pastoral theology, is driven by a solid and well-honed "inquiry of accompaniment." This method of inquiry is as pastoral as the presence of Jesus with us. It is a sacred inquiry built up intentionally from the sources of faith. As accompanists help people inquire into the experiences of their lives, they do so in a manner that is in keeping with the points of orientation and guidelines of pastoral theology: Christ at the center, a personalist approach, connected to the liturgy, recognition of the universal call to holiness and the call to self-giving love, pride of place for the tradition of the Church, a call to the Lord's cross, awareness that grace is acting, and mercy as the primary attitude.

Such a method of sacred inquiry provides a "toolbox" for authentic accompaniment. Pastoral accompanists help the person of God under their care *to interpret* their questions, experiences, pending decisions, or situations using this specific "method of inquiry." They help them interpret these parts of their lives in the light of the gospel and the teaching of the Church.

It's important to note that this method of inquiry is not a "test." It forms part of the conversation between the person of God seeking help and the accompanist. In any given chat, the accompanist may use any or none of these areas of inquiry, depending on when the time is right. This requires great patience on the part of the accompanist. Again, Pope Francis in article 171 of *The Joy of the Gospel* reminds us that

> reaching a level of maturity where individuals can make truly free and responsible decisions *calls for much time and patience*. As Blessed Peter Faber used to say: "Time is God's messenger." (italics mine)

And in article 24 of the same document he teaches:

> An evangelizing community is also supportive, standing by people at every step of the way, no matter how difficult or lengthy this may prove to be. It is familiar with patient expectation and apostolic endurance. *Evangelization consists mostly of patience and disregard for constraints of time.* (italics mine)

Accompanists always have in the back of their minds a short set of questions or areas of inquiry. By gently stepping into these areas with the seeker, the accompanist may be able to help the seeker hear God's voice, to be able to discern what God is asking of them in their real and specific situation. The accompanist must be wise enough to understand that in due time, in God's time, through the work of grace and only by grace, each seeker will come to an understanding of what God is asking of them. This isn't cookie-cutter pastoral practice where everyone gets the same treatment. This is a pastoral process guided by a clear and faithful method of inquiry, which little by little leads people to the Lord. What is that method of inquiry?

The areas of sacred inquiry

First of all, the areas of sacred inquiry are closely linked with those "sources of wisdom" that I mentioned above: Scripture, friendship with Jesus, Church teaching, culture, experience, and the conscience.

Learning this method of sacred inquiry is essential for everyone who seeks to accompany others. (The method is also very useful for one's personal spiritual journey.) Again, these are not questions posed as a sort of test, but they are areas of sacred inquiry through which accompanists help the seeker to understand what God is asking. Because these are very personal areas about which there is inquiry—areas that affect one's faith, privacy, and even security in certain situations—accompanists must be careful not to pose questions as threats, to assume a correct answer, or to show impatience even when it seems to them that nothing is moving in the heart of the seeker.

I'm going to list below the areas of inquiry that, taken together, constitute authentic accompaniment, but please note that they may not unfold in real time in this same order. Also bear in mind that these areas of inquiry necessarily overlap one another. They can be listed as distinct items here, but in reality they're very interconnected.

Moreover—and very important—the accompanist keeps a sort of formal idea in mind about the various elements of the inquiry, but it may not be necessary or helpful to speak explicitly about them all to the one seeking help. It is the task of the accompanist to monitor and track the conversation but not to dominate it and especially not to make any long speeches about the value of Church teaching or the reasons for the Church's position on this or that. Such "sermonizing" has no place in authentic accompaniment.

Once again, the overarching question in all accompaniment is to ask, "To what is God calling us at this moment?" As Pope Francis put it in *The Joy of Love*, 303, a person can come to see that a particular decision is in line with "what God himself is asking" amid the concrete complexity of one's specific situation while yet not fully the objective ideal [of the Church]. Hence the importance of this sacred inquiry and its lines of reflection.

1. Friendship with Jesus and familiarity with Scripture. The first level of inquiry has to do with how the story they're telling affects their friendship with Jesus. The accompanist keeps in mind throughout the time spent with the seeker that Jesus is walking with us, as on the road to Emmaus. It's in the Christian way of life to turn our hearts to him, to share with him from our heart and soul, from the deepest place within us. We also listen as Jesus' voice echoes in the depths of our souls. If the seeker isn't steeped so deeply in a relationship with Jesus, the accompanist can nudge him or her in that direction, even if ever so slightly.

It is also necessary for each accompanist to know Jesus Christ and to know him as Lord and companion.

Accompanists must spend time with Jesus in prayerful reflection, opening themselves to grace, speaking with Jesus as with
a friend. For what do people hunger? What selfishness continues to occur? What memories, dreams, hurts, sins, or failures
do people withhold or hide from him? What desires, urges, or
feelings do people block? To know Jesus like this, the accompanist must encounter him in the gospels, in the Eucharist,
and in the daily turning of the heart.

Pope Francis has set the stage for this in the opening
thoughts of his *The Joy of the Gospel*. There he said in article 3:

> I invite all Christians, everywhere, at this very moment,
> to a renewed personal encounter with Jesus Christ, or
> at least an openness to letting him encounter them; I
> ask all of you to do this unfailingly each day. No one
> should think that this invitation is not meant for him
> or her, since "no one is excluded from the joy brought
> by the Lord." The Lord does not disappoint those who
> take this risk; whenever we take a step towards Jesus,
> we come to realize that he is already there, waiting for
> us with open arms.

In the process of accompanying others, the accompanist
might ask simply,

- "How does this experience or decision affect your
  friendship with Jesus?"

Or, if that is too bold a question, the accompanist might ask,

- "Does any of this connect to your faith?"

- "What insights do you have about this?"

If any direct question about this seems too bold, too eager, or simply too early in your conversation, the accompanist resolves that by listening carefully to how the seeker tells the story. What elements of faith appear in it, if any? Does there seem to be a fundamental orientation toward Christ in this person's life? Do gospel values surface in the storytelling?

If no fundamental orientation toward God is apparent, it will be difficult to move forward with discernment. As I have said here several times, the goal is to assist this person (the seeker) to come to understand what God may be asking of him or her in this particular circumstance in their lives. God speaks in the depths of our souls, as the *Catechism* teaches in article 1776. So, if there is no orientation toward God, it will be difficult to hear God's voice as it sounds within the soul. It is for this reason that the accompanist begins the inquiry with this area of observation.

On the other hand, God works in marvelous ways beyond human understanding, so the accompanist rightly can continue to believe that grace will move this seeker who sits in front of him or her. Sometimes the very presence of a patient accompanist, listening with respect and offering love and mercy, becomes the turning point in the faith of the seeker. Sometimes, in fact, the orientation to God is not explicit, but it does exist, expressing itself in acts of goodness and mercy. The accompanist listens for evidence of works of mercy, acts of kindness and self-giving love, an other-centered attitude, a heart for the poor, for justice, peace, or the common good. These may indicate that this person, even though not explicit about expressing faith, is following the way of God in his or her life.

If the person seeking help has a more well-developed faith, the accompanist may help the seeker pray with the gospels. In these stories, the encounter with Jesus helps to solidify and make more intimate the seeker's connection with him. One way to enter into such an encounter is through the use of Ignatian imaginative prayer with the various stories. In this prayer, the seeker and accompanist place themselves within the story, listening to and watching what happens. They may even approach the Lord in their imaginations during a quiet moment "in the action" and speak with Jesus from their heart. Ignatius taught his monks that God speaks to us through such imaginative prayer. It's a powerful addition to the experience of accompaniment when it is appropriately used with someone whose faith is more mature.

2. The call to holiness and the Paschal Mystery. As I said above in the treatment of the guidelines for pastoral theology, Catholics believe that everyone is called to holiness. Even those who seem furthest away from explicit faith are called to holiness. This begs the question: What do we mean by the term "holiness"?

Holiness as such is an abstract idea with which most people don't identify. Some people think of the saints as holy. They might think that nuns and monks are holy but that laypeople just wander around in secular unholiness. In fact, holiness can be recognized only by its actions. It's a call to forgiveness, generosity, prayer, self-giving love, justice, and a love for the poor. It's a call to live the Beatitudes, to follow the corporal and spiritual works of mercy, and to embrace, welcome, and make use of the gifts of the Holy Spirit. It's a call to be conscious of one's sins and aware of the generous mercy with which God has treated us. We see holiness by how it's lived more than by how it's professed. As we well know, being ordained or a professed religious doesn't guarantee holiness; we're all on a journey.

In accompaniment, then, the accompanist watches and listens for signs of holiness, as we said above, even if no explicit faith is expressed. In fact, sometimes when a person proclaims his or her faith explicitly, the accompanist must be on guard, because there must also be signs of that faith in how the person *lives*. As Pope Francis has often said,[35] "Reality is more important than ideas."

In hearing the story of someone seeking help, an accompanist is asking himself or herself—or in the right setting, may even ask the seeker:

- "How is the call to holiness embedded within this situation or experience?"

How does this person live out the values of the gospel? If the accompanist sees signs that those values are being lived, then he or she knows that, at some level, there is a fundamental orientation toward goodness, justice, and love. God is actively engaged with this person in the depths of his or her soul, and this person is responding as God nudges and prods him or her toward love.

The accompanist listens to the seeker's story, holding in the back of his or her mind a pair of questions that are part of this sacred inquiry. The seeker has had a series of experiences that have yielded questions or concerns in his or her mind. The accompanist asks,

- "In which experiences is there embedded the call to love, generosity, forgiveness, a heart for the poor and the earth, and the values of Jesus and the Light?"

This is self-giving love drawing the community together in unity.

On the other hand, the accompanist must also ask,

- "In which experiences are found a rejection of goodness and a movement toward violence, hate, death, anger, aggression, cruelty, and the values of the evil one and the dark side?"

This is selfish and unilateral, causing division and polarization in the community.

As we saw clearly in our earlier discussion of the Paschal Mystery, the hallmark of the Christian life is immersion in the dying and rising of Christ. To enter into the Paschal Mystery is to die to one's self. It is to "die with him that we might rise with him." As an accompanist walks with others, he or she is attuned to this central mystery of our faith. Again, it bears repeating over and over again that we are forgiven for our selfishness and sin. We are forgiven. Period.

This is the kerygma in which the good news is so remarkable that it's difficult for us to believe. This is the point in the accompaniment process where the accompanist has a chance to announce to the seeker nothing less than this: we are forgiven because of the sacrifice Jesus made on the cross. We are forgiven. God holds nothing against us. As accompanists listen to the stories of seekers—whether painful or joyful—they inquire with them about their knowledge of this great mystery of forgiveness. For once seekers understand it, they will be able to hear their call to self-sacrifice, fidelity, kindness, gentleness, and trust in God.

Hence, the question an accompanist might ask of the seeker is about how this situation leads him or her to self-giving love and dying to self. We might ask,

- "How is God calling you to share in the cross of Christ now?" or
- "How are you called to die to yourself?"

If that's too bold a question or if the time isn't quite right for it, you can tone it down without losing the strength of the idea by asking,

- "What sacrifice of yourself does this situation call on you to make?" or
- "Of what are you called to let go?"

Accompanists must be careful when they call people to die to themselves, because some may misunderstand this as giving up one's integrity or allowing others to use them inappropriately. These latter situations are not healthy. In accompaniment, it is never appropriate to call people to behave in such a way that others may abuse or violate them or their dignity.

3. Church teachings and the Christian tradition. For such theological reflection to be truly authentic, it is important for the accompanist to know Catholic tradition well. Faith is not a private matter but a shared journey. Christians share faith with many others as well as with the entire communion of saints. Christians are, after all, the "people of God" and, as a people, there is much that they share. It is personal but never private. It is the role of an accompanist to help a seeker understand what and why the tradition teaches.

The goal of accompaniment as we have said is to help people to clarify what God is asking of them in a particular situation. It is to help them discern God's voice as it echoes in their depths, as the *Catechism* puts it in its teaching on the conscience in article 1776. The *Catechism* also spells out how accompaniment should unfold or how a person should go about forming his or her conscience. In article 1785, the *Catechism* says this:

> In the formation of conscience, the Word of God is the light for our path; we must assimilate it in faith and prayer and put it into practice. We must also examine our conscience before the Lord's Cross. We are assisted by the gifts of the Holy Spirit, aided by the witness or advice of others, and guided by the authoritative teaching of the Church.

This leads pastoral theology to take seriously all the Church teaches and apply it to the ministry of accompaniment as much as possible. This line of inquiry addresses that. It's important for the accompanist to know well what the Church teaches, to know Catholic traditions and customs. One way to do that is by the use of the *Catechism of the Catholic Church*. As we saw in article 1785 above, the one seeking help will be "guided" by the teaching of the Church. However, this seeker may very well not know what the teachings are, and this is where the accompanist plays a vital role.

One way to step gently into this part of the conversation is to simply ask,

- "Do you know what we teach about this?" or
- "Have you thought about how you will reconcile your experience or decision with Church teaching?"

The *Catechism* itself may not make for easy reading, so having on hand another resource will be a great benefit to the accompanist.

The key concern when introducing Church teaching is to be sure that the seeker knows precisely and accurately what the Church teaches. Many adults have not had any religious education since their secondary school confirmation program. It is important for the accompaniment process that how Church teaching is introduced be thoroughly pastoral. The original wording of the *Catechism* can sometimes be difficult for people to understand or integrate. The *Catechism* itself is not meant to be a textbook; it's meant to be a reliable source for teachers and pastoral ministers. It can be a help to seekers to present them with Church teaching in a more "plain English" or "español común" version of the *Catechism*.[36]

4. Scrutiny of the signs of the times and the culture. Accompanists must also learn to consult and scrutinize what is happening around them in the world, the so-called signs of the times. What advances in human understanding emerge from medicine, psychology, sociology, and other areas of human endeavor? God continues to reveal the divine plan to humans in these discoveries. What do people read in the daily news? What's happening in one's family? One's culture? The cultures of others around the world?

In certain Christian circles, the signs of the times are an indication of the end of the world. These Christians read war, famine, disease, and natural disasters as signs of the "end times." But for Catholics and many other Christians, the mandate is to become aware of what's happening around us so that we can interpret those events in light of the gospel.

It is necessary for an accompanist to become a person who understands the times. Karl Barth often said it was necessary to have the Bible in one hand and the newspaper in the other. With this in mind, we might ask, what divine call is embedded in the advances being made in science and medicine? What do we hear in the news that informs or challenges our faith? How should we respond to the well-known reality of the people who have been impoverished around the world? To dying children? To the destruction of the environment? What have we learned in psychology and sociology that might help us as the family of God?

What do all these "signs of the times" say to us Christians and Catholics? This is important to us because, frankly, these are the times in which we—the people of God—are living. We aren't living in the 1950s any longer, for example, or the 1560s.

But to scrutinize the times is not like reading off a thermometer. Getting it right is difficult. One way to approach this quandary is to enter into prayerful theological reflection and inquire of the times just as we do of people's experiences. We might ask how this or that development or situation informs our lives of faith? Does this new knowledge or understanding reflect the teaching of Jesus and the gospels?

For example, how does advancing human knowledge in medicine and psychology inform what we teach now about birth control, same-sex relationships, capital punishment, the care of the earth, the place and role of women, or marriage and married people in ministry? Or in another example, how do our advances in ecumenism inform how we treat non-Catholic parents, non-Catholic spouses, neighboring mosques, synagogues, or Protestant churches? In a third example, how does our understanding of what Jesus teaches in Matthew 25 inform our thinking about immigrants today in our society? How does it inform how we help the poor and the homeless? How does Jesus' encounter with the rich young man inform what we do with our own money?

In September 2015, Pope Francis commented[37] on how to read the signs of the times. It helps to be careful, he said, not to condemn everything we encounter in the modern world. We should not assume that everything "was better in the past" or seek refuge in fixed ways of thinking or fundamentalism. Openness to what medicine, psychology, or other sciences and human effort are teaching us helps us in our work of pastoral theology. On the other hand, Pope Francis warned, we should not consecrate everything as though every new movement or idea should be embraced. We should not, he said, reject all the lessons we have learned in our history, "in our rich ecclesial history," as he put it.

"The path to overcoming these temptations," he said, "lies in reflection, discernment, and taking both the ecclesiastical tradition and current reality very seriously, placing them in dialogue with one another." This is the role of prayerful theological reflection. What we discern in this reflection cannot contradict the content of the message we have received. But as Pope Francis reminds us in this same speech,

> Doctrine is not a closed, private system deprived of dynamics able to raise questions and doubts. On the contrary, Christian doctrine has a face, a body, flesh: He is called Jesus Christ, and it is his life that is offered from generation to generation to all men [and women] and in all places.

Balancing the times with the tradition

Finally, a word is needed regarding the relationship between two of our sources: (1) the signs of the times and (2) the current teachings of the Church. It's true that over time, Church teaching develops. As we said above, new advances in medicine, psychology, and sociology sometimes shed new light on the questions and experiences people face and how the Church responds to them. Likewise, cultural change can affect how an individual or the official magisterium of the Church itself understands the seeker's situation in life.

As we reach points of consensus about what the signs of the times may mean for us in pastoral theology, we are careful to apply certain criteria[38] to our conclusions. First, does this connect with the long tradition of the Church, and if not, why and how can we accept it? We have, of course, changed course on various questions, such as slavery, usury, capital punishment, and others, but our reasons for advancing to new understandings must show an integral connection to our faith. Second, does our conclusion lead to the values of the gospel and the Church: to holiness, justice, goodness, love, forgiveness, and generosity? No rightly made conclusion can ever lead to values contrary to the gospel, such as hate, racism, greed, lust, envy, or idolatry. Third, can our conclusion be properly taken with us into the liturgy? Can we celebrate and pray about this? For example, it is impossible to imagine praying at Sunday Mass that the immigrants who are seeking a home among us be shunned, turned away, and separated from their children, even if the signs of the times point to that being the case. It would not jive with the liturgy we pray. And finally, is our conclusion open to the input and evaluation of the larger church, or is this a private conclusion made only to benefit ourselves?

The accompanist should take care to avoid either of two extremes in this regard. First, the accompanist should not disregard or criticize Church teaching when it is in conflict with the seeker's experience. What the Church teaches about birth control, for example, remains valid and important. Embedded in that teaching are key values for the married couple that help them achieve mutual love, an open heart to children, and the care of their bodies. On the other hand, the experience and discernment about this by hundreds and thousands of modern couples should inform the magisterium of the Church, and evaluation of this teaching should be considered.

Second, if a particular seeker reaches a conclusion in his or her conscience that varies from Church teaching on this or any matter, provided once again that the decision does not lead to hatred, violence, death, or other values contrary to the gospel, the accompanist should also avoid criticizing the seeker, lecturing him or her on Church teaching, or warning them of dire spiritual consequences. The role of the accompanist is to walk with but not dominate the seeker in his or her discernment. It's a delicate balancing act.

The art of sacred inquiry, in sum

[a] Friendship with Jesus and familiarity with Scripture. Any Christian who is seeking to discern what God is asking of him or her begins here. The two avenues into this source are (1) prayer in which we are in conversation and dialogue with Jesus in our daily lives, and (2) the stories and anecdotes of the gospels in which we meet the Lord in his pastoral ministry.

[b] The call to holiness and the Lord's cross. This is a call to die to oneself out of self-giving love for others. It's a profound call embedded in the situations, people, and experiences around us. It is embedded, in short, in daily human experience.

[c] The teachings of the Church and the Christian tradition. We are all members of the family or community of God. We do not go to the heart of the Lord alone. The Church has a body of doctrine, law, and moral codes that guide us along the way. Again, there are two avenues into this source. The first is the formal, official teaching of the Church as found in the *Catechism* or a suitable version of it in plainer English. The second is the liturgy of the Church in which we encounter the Lord in the context of the body of Christ.

[d] The signs of the times. People live within a given culture and society, and where they live affects the experiences, situations, or questions they bring to accompaniment. As the human family advances in its understandings of the human situation, people trail along, picking up this or shunning that. Especially in matters of love and how people form their adult households, current cultural change—and we always take

that with a grain of salt—significantly affects them, and it's necessary to carefully balance the times with the tradition.

STEP 6: THE MOMENT OF THEOLOGICAL REFLECTION: CONTEMPLATION

As we consult these various sources and pass through the process of accompaniment, the seeker and accompanist bring all these elements into a lively dialogue with each other to learn from them. Gradually the seeker must take them into his or her interior space, his or her mind and heart. The accompanist can help the seeker learn to listen with an inner ear and to see anew with the mind's eye. Once seekers have consulted and come to know these sources, they can open themselves to the divine source deep within their conscience. They reflect with an intentional openness to God, present in the person of Jesus Christ and made known by the Holy Spirit. In a word, they are open to the Holy. Seekers and accompanists both assume a contemplative stance and learn to place themselves in a receptive posture that leads to discernment.

There is an ongoing discussion in pastoral ministry circles about whether or not it is appropriate at some point in the accompaniment process to invite the seeker to explicit, verbal prayer. The accompanist, of course, should be attentive to the presence of Jesus and his desires for us. But to ask the seeker to pray, especially if he or she is somewhat new to this process, may end up driving them away from future encounters.

STEP 7: DISCERNMENT AND DECISION

Once the accompanist has heard the story, understood it, and begun the gentle sacred inquiry, he or she moves into discernment. This is done without any fanfare or announcements. The accompanist simply begins listening to his or her own heart to detect what response he or she has to the story and the seeker. This "listening to the heart" begins for the accompanist at the same time that discernment is beginning in the seeker's heart. It's important to note that the accompanist is not discerning on behalf of the seeker but is listening to how God is leading him or her as the agent in the accompaniment process. This dual discernment process continues for as long as needed. The accompanist might ask the seeker, for example:

- "What insights do you have about this?"
- "What does your heart tell you about this?"

If the seeker is a person of faith, the accompanist might ask:

- "What do you hear Jesus calling you to do or be in this situation?"
- "What do you hear in your conscience about this?

Clarity

As people learn the art of discernment, they realize that, when they listen to their conscience, they're listening to God. But often in modern life, there is a lot of noise—advertising, media, people, demands in the schedule, or more media. How can seekers and accompanists trust that it is God's voice they hear? Elijah had the same question. Elijah was doing some discernment when he experienced a God-given inner urge to go out and stand on a high mountain before the Lord. He had a strong sense that the Lord was calling him, and he was listening intently for the Lord's voice. In a sense, accompaniment is a moment in the life of the seekers when they, like Elijah, stop what they're doing and sit with someone who can help them hear. As he listened, however, Elijah was in for a surprise. Here's the text from 1 Kings 19.

"Now there was a great wind," the text tells us. It was "so strong that it was splitting the mountains…but the Lord was not in the wind; and after the wind an earthquake, but the Lord was not in the earthquake; and after the earthquake a fire, but the Lord was not in the fire; and after the fire, a sound of sheer silence" (11–12).

Sheer silence. When Elijah heard this silence, "he wrapped his face in his mantle and went out and stood at the entrance of the cave" (13a). And it was then and there that he heard God's voice. The first step in discernment, then, is to listen as God speaks in the silence of the human heart, and this requires that the seeker and accompanist pause to listen, that they set aside some quiet and alone time for self-examination and introspection.

To reach this point in discernment in the context of pastoral accompaniment requires—on the part of both the accompanist and the one seeking help—a fundamental and radical openness to hearing the voice of God. Theological reflection allows both seeker and accompanist to ponder how and where they meet God, as Elijah did. This prayerful moment—a combination of contemplation and discernment—requires that both participants be able to center themselves and maintain an interior space of quiet and stillness. One role of the accompanist is to assist the seeker in learning this listening posture. Once learned, the seeker can trust the discernment wholeheartedly.

There is, however, an exception to this rule. If the seeker is among the very self-assured whom we discussed above, and appears to be reaching a conclusion that violates another person, is composed of hate or hateful prejudice, threatens the sanctity of life, or is blind to the sources, especially to friendship with Jesus, then the accompanist may need to take action. What action? Even though the journey underway belongs to the seeker and the seeker alone, one's conscience is formed by consulting "the witness or advice of others" (*Catechism*, 1785). In these cases—and this should be a rare experience—the accompanist gives the seeker feedback to discourage his or her plan of action. If the accompanist learns that there is abuse or violence involved, then it must be reported to the proper authorities.

Accompanists benefit from opening their hearts to allow Jesus to walk with them in these moments of discernment. It leads to the experience of being mindful of Jesus' presence without necessarily proclaiming him from the rooftops. This is the time to turn one's heart to the Holy Spirit and allow the Spirit to give the accompanist the grace of awareness and faith. The accompanist asks for the insight needed to understand his or her role in this situation. The words needed for healing will come at the right moment.

As we said above and are repeating for good pedagogy, the context for this accompaniment and discernment varies. It could be in the sacrament of reconciliation in which the penitent shares his or her story, and the priest minister accompanies him or her to God's mercy. It could be in a formal conversation between pastoral minister and parishioner in the parish office. It could be parent interviews for those whose children are preparing for the first celebrations of the sacraments. It could be within the family, one intentionally helping another. It could be during marriage preparation, in moments of bereavement, during pastoral care visits to a hospital or nursing home, in a youth group setting, in a parish-based retreat, during recruitment of catechists, when two spouses routinely sit down for morning coffee to chat, or in many other contexts. This is the role that a sponsor should play in confirmation or the RCIA, or a godparent after baptism. The context could be an ongoing series of accompaniment chats or a single, one-time chat along the way, as it was for the two people walking out to Emmaus.

What these contexts have in common is the intention of listening to God, of discerning what God is asking of a particular person in a concrete situation. In any of these contexts, it helps if both the seeker and the accompanist "turn down the lights" on the busyness of life and move to quiet reflection, setting aside the time needed for this journey inward. It helps if they can "turn down the volume" of their own thoughts and shift to a somewhat contemplative posture, listening as Elijah did. Both the seeker and accompanist can learn to gaze at Jesus and allow Jesus to gaze back at them, as the Curé of Ars put it. They become aware of any prejudices they may bring to this, any lost dreams or memories, anything they may repress or deny, any of life's "winds, earthquakes, or fires," indeed, anything that might prevent them from hearing the Lord speak to them. The participants in accompaniment learn to listen for the intuition that arises in their souls about the situation or question at hand. What call is embedded in it? What healing word do they hear? What words of mercy and compassion and forgiveness do they hear?

In short, what sense of consolation or desolation do the participants experience in the discernment process?

Consolation and Desolation

Vinita Hampton Wright[39] has written beautifully about how to recognize consolation and desolation in the discernment process. These two very important poles of consciousness help persons in discernment know whether they are following the way of the Lord or not. The seeker and accompanist must pay attention to these as they work through theological reflection and discernment.

In general, desolation is experienced as emptiness, hopelessness, and a sense that something is not right. In the words of Vinita Wright, we might say that a person dwells in a state of desolation when she or he is "moving away from God's active presence in the world. We know we are moving in this way when we sense the growth of resentment, ingratitude, selfishness, doubt, fear, and so on. If my outlook becomes increasingly gloomy and self-obsessed, I am in a state of desolation. I am resisting God or, if not actively resisting, I am being led away from God by other influences." When people experience desolation, they also notice that they have turned in on themselves, paying attention to their own needs and wants above those of others. It separates them from the community of God and makes them want to give up on things that they know they're called to do when they're "in their right mind."

On the other hand, consolation moves the seeker very near the heart of the Lord. A person dwells in a state of consolation when she or he is "moving toward God's active presence in the world." One can trust that he or she is moving in this direction when they sense the growth of love or faith or mercy or hope—or any qualities we know as gifts of the Holy Spirit.

Consolation may fool a person. It doesn't imply that they have reached a state of absolute happiness. In fact, what people discern may well be costly to them. It may demand that they give away their time, money, or personal space. They may be called to undertake works of mercy, to forgive seventy times seven times, or to carry a cross up a mountain. Or perhaps they will be called to well-earned rest after many years of hard work, to enjoy the presence of God's love, or to enjoy a time of play and recreation. They may be called to speak a word of comfort, to move beyond their comfort zones, or to speak up in the face of injustice and falsehood. God calls people to many and varied tasks and places. When the seeker and accompanist sense that they're on the right road—the pathway of the Lord—they can follow it with trust. Consolation brings with it renewed energy, peace, and sense of community. Ideas flow and one's mind is clear.

In theological reflection, accompanists may experience within themselves either of these spiritual states—consolation or desolation—or they may observe them in the person seeking their help.

Decision
In time, accompaniment and discernment lead to decisions. The accompanist helps the seeker to choose a direction. It could be the sacrament of reconciliation, an AA or Al-Anon group, or even treatment if needed. Sometimes the action might involve an apology when that's in order. Sometimes it will mean an appointment to start the annulment process at

the matrimonial tribunal in the diocese. Other times it may mean some ongoing spiritual direction or more sessions for coaching and accompaniment.

It's often possible to reach a point of genuine consolation in discernment quite rapidly if the case is clear or if the shared discernment and wisdom of others has helped the seeker reach a conclusion.

STEP 8: HEALING AND RESTORATION

The outcome of prayerful theological reflection closely reflects the ministry of Jesus and leads to healing. Accompanists want to do more than merely gain clarity or new insights. This isn't an exercise in psychoanalysis or any sort of therapy. The primary goal is a faith response. Accompanists want to bring faith to bear on life experiences to come to a new way of perceiving and a new way of responding,[40] which leads to healing and integration.

This healing and integration may take many forms, including but not limited to celebrating sacramentally and sharing meals. As in the story of the prodigal, it also includes being incorporated into the community anew, which reflects the sacramental and dining experiences of the Lord. How will this happen? Prayerful theological reflection always lands the seeker and accompanist somewhere on *terra firma*. Seekers are real, concrete persons living in real time and space, so the healing finds a concrete way of expressing itself as well.

In the parish, this process can offer tremendous healing to people unless, in the end, the parish refuses to integrate the person or family. Allowing people to tell their stories carries a risk. What if the story they tell is filled with darkness and sin? How will the accompanist respond? Since people's stories are often painful and difficult, accompanists must learn to touch the sores of the leper and assure people of God's forgiveness. For a parish to integrate or restore a person to full life in the community, a plan should be in place, and leaders should consider all diocesan regulations before inviting people to make this journey.

— AN ILLUSTRATION —

Wally and Helen

When Wally and Helen came to see Janice, their parish associate, they were terrified for the eternal salvation of their nephew who had died by suicide a month earlier. He was a young man, only seventeen, and his death was completely unexpected. He left behind a note, but the note only explained that he did this to save his parents the embarrassment of having a gay son. His parents were stunned both by this announcement as well as by his irreversible action. When Trevor told them he was gay, about six months before this, they had asked if he was certain about it, and showing embarrassment, they asked him not to tell others. They tried to be as accepting as they could be, but they had both supported a ban on gay marriage in their state, and Trevor knew this. "His coming out was difficult for his parents too," Helen told Janice. Now they realize they should have been more loving toward him.

All the other issues aside, Helen and Wally came to Janice seeking some assurance. They weren't sure, but they thought they remembered that suicide was a mortal sin and that people who died in the act could not go to heaven. Helen and Wally wanted to give a word of comfort to their sister and brother-in-law, but they weren't sure what to say.

Janice was a skilled accompanist. She first let them tell their story, nudging them here or there for an explanatory detail and listening with the ears of God. They poured out the whole story, each of them interrupting the other with notes of sadness and confusion. Janice could see that the people in front of her were people of great faith, so she felt she could gently ask about their view of what Jesus might think of their nephew's decision and action.

"I think he would be terribly sad," Helen said. "He'd be just as sad as we are. But I don't think he would punish Trevor," she said. Trevor had already suffered greatly from bullying in his school and from the fear of being unloved, they told her. Religious and political leaders had also frightened him by condemnations and stereotypes reported in the press. Like many young people, he internalized those negative messages, and his fatal decision to end his life was a way out of all that, Helen told Janice, while Wally nodded along.

Slowly, Janice invited Helen and Wally to express their grief, their concern for their sister, and their confusion about what happens now for Trevor. She asked Helen and Wally if they understood about same-sex orientations. They answered that they had read up on it after Trevor came out. It's no longer considered any sort of psychological illness but a normal and recurring orientation for a significant percentage of people, they told her.

Janice next turned to the suicide itself. She could see that Helen and Wally had not studied the teaching of the Church for quite a while. She felt it would help if she cited Church teaching on suicide, so she told them that, yes, it is wrong for a person to do this. It is the taking of a life. But she had at hand the full teaching of the Church, which speaks of mercy and mitigating circumstances. She shared it with Helen and Wally. In part, it says:

> At the same time, the pastors of the Church recognize that sometimes people face seemingly insurmountable life situations, suffer from mental illness, give up hope for one reason or another, or fear hardship or torture. We trust in God's mercy above all, and we hope and pray for those who do this, but we do not condemn them.[41]

"We trust in God's mercy..." Helen read aloud as she moved her finger along the page. "We pray for those who do this, but we do not condemn them." There was a long silence as these words hung in the air. Janice sensed in the silence that Helen and Wally were relieved and had new hope again. Janice then moved to the next step with them and asked what they planned to do next about this. Helen and Wally were stumped. "I don't know," Wally said. "Do we have to do something else?" Before Janice could answer him, Helen spoke up.

"I'm going back to see Trevor's mom and dad," she said.

"What will you tell them?" Janice asked.

"I'm going to say that God loves their son very much, even now. I'm going to tell them that the parish is praying for Trevor and that death cannot break the bonds of love. And I'm going to tell her that I love them, that we love them. That we'll stand with them and get through this. It may take some time, and we may always regret what Trevor did, but eventually, we'll get through it."

"Does that seem OK with you, Wally?" Janice asked him.

"To be honest, I was thinking the same thing," he said. "We can't just stay away from them. We can't holler at them for how they treated Trevor. They already feel pretty bad about all this, so I think Helen is right." He took her hand. "As sad as this whole thing is," he concluded, "it would be worse if we went silent."

As their time together came to a close, Janice invited Helen and Wally to return for another visit if they wanted to. She didn't instigate verbal prayer with them because she sensed they wouldn't be comfortable with it, but she did offer to include Trevor in the prayer of the faithful for the following Sunday. She had accompanied this couple through a dark night in their lives, or at least through an hour or two of the darkness, but she had also left them with legitimate hope and light. Like many people do, they found their own way out of the forest with an accompanist's help.

Evaluation

Later, Janice reported that it was a great comfort to Helen and Wally that she could lead them in a brief reflection that brought together all the sources mentioned above: friendship with Jesus, the call to holiness and dying to self, and the teaching of the Church. She felt she properly blended these sources with "the signs of the times" regarding new understandings of what it means to be homosexual today. Janice reported that once she heard Helen speak of Jesus the way she did, she knew that Helen was experiencing consolation in her faith. Helen's heart was lifted, allowing her to sense the closeness of Jesus as well as his compassion. Janice's only task was to affirm Helen in her faith.

Janice knew that her time with Helen and Wally was most likely very limited; she would see them this one time, and not for longer than an hour or so. Therefore, without rushing them, she moved along in accompanying them to try to conclude with a plan of action within that first chat.

Janice also reported later that having on hand and being very conversant with the teachings of the Church as presented in the *Catechism* was essential. "Many people don't know what we teach," she told me. "They're guessing. And most of the time they guess that we're much harsher and more judgmental than we really are." The turning point for Helen and Wally was knowing that the Church, like Jesus, does not condemn Trevor, that it has mercy on him, that mitigating circumstances are surely what drove him to this fatal decision.

Review

- **The principal activity** of pastoral theology is a form of prayerful theological reflection drawing on the sources that include (1) Scripture and friendship with Jesus, (2) the teaching of the Church, and (3) the signs of the times.
- **The context** for the reflection is accompaniment. A person seeking help brings a concrete situation or experience, a question, decision, or concern to the pastoral accompanist and asks for help.
- **The accompanist**—with ears open to the seeker and heart open to Jesus—invites the seeker to tell his or her story and listens with an active, nonjudgmental

heart. For the accompanist, this is the first stage of the prayerful theological reflection.

- **The art of inquiry.** Slowly the accompanist inquires about the matter at hand, following a somewhat formal-yet-informal "hermeneutic or inquiry of accompaniment," bringing to bear all three of the sources.

- **Discernment for the seeker.** Using however much time is needed or available—it could be a few hours or several months or many years—the accompanist slowly helps the seeker discern what God may be asking of him or her in that particular moment. This discernment shows signs along the way of either consolation or desolation on the part of the seeker. The accompanist is attuned to this holy activity. The work of discernment belongs to the seeker, not the accompanist.

- **Discernment for the accompanist.** However, the accompanist is also in a process of sacred discernment, listening to his or her own heart about what is happening, trusting the nudges and intuitions that may assist the process.

- **Decision.** At some reasonable point, the accompanist assists the seeker to reach a point of decision and action, which may lead to integration in the parish. This may conclude the accompaniment relationship for them.

- **Evaluation.** Afterward, the accompanist and his or her colleagues evaluate and appraise the experience and process. Accompanists do not act alone but in league with others.

PART SIX

Becoming a Parish of Promise and Hope

SECTION 1: THE PARISH IS THE CONTEXT

In many parishes today there is a large number of people who are no longer present. Social commentators and demographers like to refer to people with no church affiliation as "nones" or "ex-Catholics." From pastoral theology, however, a better name for them might be "not yet made to feel fully welcome" or "not yet listened to." We Catholics believe that everyone has an inborn hunger to connect with God, and that connection to the divine is rarely made alone. For this reason, the parish, when it is a refuge of listening and compassionate ministry, remains a vital neighborhood presence, and the renewal in pastoral theology can make it stronger.

> The parish is not an outdated institution; precisely because it possesses great flexibility, it can assume quite different contours depending on the openness and missionary creativity of the pastor and the community.
> THE JOY OF THE GOSPEL, 28

Parishes are the context in which most pastoral ministry is enacted. Therefore, they must continually align and realign themselves with the points of orientation that are the foundation of pastoral theology. All members of the parish, whether in the common or ministerial priesthoods, have co-responsibility for making sure the work of Jesus in today's world is accomplished in their particular local community, which is the parish. A parish examen based on those points of orientation can help to reveal in which areas a given parish may need to make that alignment defined and evident in order to become a true parish of promise and hope. The promise is mercy, always mercy. And the hope is in Christ—that we may be a strong community of love and care.

If the Church—the people of God—is to keep this promise and offer this hope, then certain steps can be taken to move down that road. These steps do not lead to any new programs. This isn't parish renewal, strictly speaking, but a shift in the attitude of the parish members who enact pastoral ministry. The shift is away from being content with the status quo to feeling the urgency of acting toward people as Jesus did. And how did Jesus treat people? As we have seen earlier in this text, he met them out on the streets and in their homes. He looked on them with mercy. He led them to discern the voice of God as it echoed within their consciences. He freely shared the table with them, whether they were sinners or not. He called them, finally, to have a greater and more self-giving love, as he did on the cross, to walk daily with him, to discern his voice in their consciences, and to turn away from all that is selfish and sinful, one step at a time.

This is the work of pastoral ministry today. It is the goal of all accompaniment. We want to act as Jesus did. In fact, we want to act like Jesus, in place of Jesus, and with the hands and voice of Jesus.

This can happen only when we accompany one another on the road, as Jesus did those disciples on the walk out to Emmaus. It's the accompaniment he taught us as he chatted with the woman at the well. It's how he patiently guided his disciples to understand what it means to die to self, to love their enemies, to serve others, and to trust in his word. Again, the whole enterprise of accompaniment takes place primarily in the context of the parish. This is where we must focus our attention.

SECTION 2: FORMS OF ACCOMPANIMENT

It's important to mention here that accompaniment—whether in the parish or outside of it—is a *skill* that people learn ("the art of accompaniment") and that is added to their current role or way of being with others. In a parish, this skill is added to homilizing, catechizing, enacting pastoral care, welcoming, and so forth. It's a skill or an art but *not a new program of any kind.* The beauty of learning the skill of accompaniment is that it makes both pastoral work in the parish as well as daily life with our friends, spouses, children, and parents much more holy. It adds a layer of mercy and compassion to every encounter we have. It's also naturally part of how people want to treat each other so the steps needed to prepare people for this are not giant ones.

Accompaniment is, after all, something parents do with their kids, spouses with each other, and all of us with aging parents. It's how we walk with friends, neighbors, and even co-workers. When Pope Francis calls us to become "spirit-filled evangelizers" (chapter 5 of *The Joy of the Gospel*) this is what he's talking about: to accompany one another in such a way that we grow in love and holiness. It is a skill that people can learn and use in everyday as well as in parish life. Yes, we can all learn how to do this kind of theological reflection and discernment. This is not meant only for an ecclesial elite or the ordained. It's meant for every Christian.

Of course, accompaniment is also how parish leaders approach the people in the pews. Hence, we will consider what forms accompaniment takes in the parish. We accompany one another in various ways depending on in what part of parish life we encounter each other. Accompaniment in the parish may take one of four common forms.

Form 1: Household relationship accompaniment

Accompaniment may occur, as I said earlier, when someone wishes to examine their primary household relationship, often but not always a marriage, to bring it into line with canon law. (a) When there is need for an annulment after a divorce, the specific goal of such accompaniment is usually short term. Well-run matrimonial tribunals may provide such accompaniment, but it may also occur outside the external forum of the tribunal in the internal forum of the conscience. In this case, the sacrament of reconciliation is the usual context for accompaniment. In some cases, the couple may not be ready for the sacrament but may begin their journey with a pastoral accompanist. (b) If there is no need for an annulment, then accompaniment of this sort serves to help a couple reconcile their household lifestyle with what the Church teaches as well as with their own conscience. Here the duration of accompaniment may also be relatively brief. The goal is to help a couple come to see what God is asking of them in the concrete circumstance of their relationship. In these cases, the couple—with the help of an accompanist—considers mitigating circumstances, gradualism, and the situation of the household, especially when there are children involved. The teaching of the Church must be considered very seriously in the discernment process.

Two quick points regarding these cases. First, remember what we said earlier—that all accompaniment has as its goal to help people grow closer to Jesus and love the Church. Hence, in both of these cases—when there is divorce or when there is not—that goal is central. Any actions or decisions rendered in the discernment process must lead the couple to this goal. Second, in either of these cases, when the need dictates this, a referral may be made for long-term spiritual direction or even therapy. Pastoral accompanists should be prepared to provide such a referral.

Form 2: Faith formation accompaniment

Outside of those primary household relationships, the second level of accompaniment common in parishes is connected to the faith formation programs of the parish. It is to offer parishioners an opportunity to chat with an accompanist on a short-term basis to help make more explicit what God may be asking of them in their particular situation as their children grow in faith. This might be offered, for example, (a) to parents with children preparing for the sacraments, or (b) to parents of the children in religious education, or (c) to couples preparing for marriage, or (d) to confirmation candidates. These chats focus, not on the parish or its programs or policies, but on the life of the seeker. The occasion for these is the preparation for the sacrament. The process is one of storytelling. The seeker is invited to share with another Christian his or her story, to peer into it a bit more deeply and hear how God may be calling them.

Great good comes out of these accompaniment chats. For one thing, people who experience them report time and again that the chat is the first time anyone in the parish has ever asked about their faith experience. The result is a strong feeling of inclusion, acceptance, and care. This greatly affects the experience of their child in formation, the preparation for marriage, or the power of the Spirit in confirmation. The power of storytelling alone drives the outcome of the chat as people become aware of new insights, realize how welcome they are in the parish, sense freedom to express their faith, and feel heard and loved by the accompanist. These accompaniment chats rarely result in a referral to anyone else. The accompanist in these cases is almost always a pastoral accompanist who has been trained to listen and assist with discernment as people's stories unfold.

Form 3: Pastoral care accompaniment

The third form of accompaniment in the parish responds to people's felt needs for help as they sort out the events or decisions of their lives and reconcile them with their faith. Such accompaniment might occur, for example, (a) during bereavement, (b) as part of what the parish offers during Lent to help people deepen their faith, (c) as an element of a parish-based retreat, (d) in the year after confirmation to youth in the parish, (e) with parishioners at large who seek such help, (f) with the priest in the sacrament of reconciliation, (g) during routine hospital or nursing home visits, or (h) in other forms of pastoral care. The accompanist will typically be a pastoral accompanist who has been trained to walk with others in this way.

Many households in any given parish go through periods of difficulty and stress when caring for aging parents, dealing with dementia, aiding and walking with people suffering from terminal illness, or other such human conditions. With great sensitivity to the suffering and pain these households endure, accompanists should always address the household—first and foremost—from the point of view of the most urgent need, regardless whether there is divorce, remarriage, cohabitation, same-sex unions, or civil marriage. As a field hospital would do, the first step is to treat the wounds. Later if appropriate, accompaniment may address other issues.

In some situations, such as when there is addiction, abuse, violence, clinical depression, or other conditions of the human spirit, accompaniment must always address the primary needs first. In many of these cases the accompanist must help guide the household to get help from outside sources, such as dependency treatment, legal recourse, medical aid, psychological therapy, or other healing arts.

Form 4: Parish-wide accompaniment

The fourth form of accompaniment is more difficult to name and describe. It is that the overall message or what we might call "the voice" of the parish must be consistently companionable for a parish-wide experience of accompaniment. This form of accompaniment is more subtle than the first three because it doesn't involve a specific accompanist. In this sense, the parish at large *becomes the accompanist*. What it says and does—as well as what the universal Church says and does—shapes the experience of each member. What message does your parish send to the members? It is welcoming and gracious or closed and severe? The message you send is contained in every homily, every announcement, every word on the website, and every case where you are called on to offer mercy.

In an accompanying parish, for example, leaders pay special attention to the office hours of the parish, as well as when the doors of the church are open and unlocked. Can everyone manage to fit their needs into the parish office schedule? Parish leaders also pay attention to the front desk and who sits there. Is the first face a visitor sees and the first voice he or she hears friendly or frightening? Are visitors a bother to the team or are they welcomed warmly? Is there a clubby feeling among those who know each other well in the parish? Do long-time members exclude newcomers and their ideas and contributions? Who answers the parish phones? If it's an automatic answering system, that may very well leave people feeling unattended to, especially if English is not their first language. Is the parish website up-to-date and friendly?

How are the signs that welcome and direct folks written? How inclusive are the announcements and written material used in the parish or on the web? We know that language creates reality and what we say matters. Each of these elements of parish life demonstrates our care for the people. The "voice" or constant message of the parish should be, "We are here for you. We do not judge you or your situation in life. You can trust us to accompany you to healing, inclusion, the sacraments, and faith formation. Whatever has happened in your life, we do not condemn you. You belong to us because you belong to Christ."

Pope Francis has coached us all regarding such matters. In *The Joy of the Gospel*, 47, he has this to say:

> The Church is called to be the house of the Father, with doors always wide open. One concrete sign of such openness is that our church doors should always be open so that if someone, moved by the Spirit, comes there looking for God, he or she will not find a closed door. There are other doors that should not be closed either. Everyone can share in some way in the life of the Church; everyone can be part of the community, nor should the doors of the sacraments be closed for simply any reason. This is especially true of the sacrament which is itself "the door": baptism. The

> Eucharist, although it is the fullness of sacramental
> life, is not a prize for the perfect but a powerful medi-
> cine and nourishment for the weak. These convictions
> have pastoral consequences that we are called to con-
> sider with prudence and boldness.

Even though this fourth form of accompaniment is more subtle than the first three, it is vitally important to the over-all success of accompaniment as yours becomes a parish of promise and hope.

SECTION 3: MOVING YOUR PARISH TOWARD ACCOMPANIMENT

What is happening in the parish today? Many times, success in parish life is measured "by the numbers." If the number of weekend communions is high, if weekly collections meet the budget, and if there are still children lining up to receive first communion, then the parish sees itself as successful. It's cer-tainly important to serve the people with all of these various offerings and programs, but Catherine Clifford[42] echoes Pope Francis when she writes:

> According to the principles that Pope Francis has
> laid out, these are "worldly" measures of success and
> not the true measure of divine grace. He invites us to
> ask instead, have the poor and the wounded found
> a home here? Are the members of this community
> being formed to be the "spirit-filled evangelizers" that
> the world needs? Is this community fully engaged in
> serving the needs of the poor and broken in the wider

neighborhood? Is this parish a place that radiates the
joy and mercy of the gospel?

Serving the poor and wounded, providing people who will
invite and welcome in Jesus' name (which is what being an
evangelizer means), serving the poor and broken in the neighborhood, and radiating joy and mercy: these are big goals for
any parish. I remind you again that achieving these goals requires a personalist approach. We serve the poor when we
reach out to specific persons who are wounded and suffering. We invite specific people to know Christ. We offer mercy
and compassion to specific persons in their real, concrete
situations. This isn't a mere philosophical theology but one
grounded in the daily lives of the people around us. And this
isn't aimed at a general, anonymous crowd but at *individuals*
who gather to form church. What steps can a parish take to
move in this direction?

Step 1. Learn together. The first step for most parishes will be
to set aside some time to study recent apostolic exhortations
such as *The Joy of the Gospel* and *The Joy of Love*, this text, and
other resources related to pastoral theology and accompaniment. The goal is to learn together what is needed to proceed
as a parish. One way to approach these texts is to read them in
small groups, sharing with and supporting one another as you
go. Another way is to use a method known as "learn and teach."
In this method, you would divide the material into small sections and, likewise, divide your team or volunteer group into
small groups. Assign one section to each small group and ask
them to learn the material together well enough that they can
teach it to the rest of your team or even to the whole parish. In

the teaching, ask each member of the group to share how their own faith is touched by their particular section, as well as how these ideas might be introduced to the parish at large.

It isn't necessary to spend a long time in this study. Most parishes can move through this material within a month or two. As you proceed, people will immediately begin stepping forward to enact the ministry, sensing their call and their gifts. But before you begin, there is a second step that it's helpful to take.

Step 2. Decide together. The second step is for the parish itself to make an actual *decision* to become a parish of accompaniment. This decision must begin with the pastor but not be limited to him. It should involve the parish council, if there is one, or other groups of leaders within the parish. Why not bring all leaders into this conversation? Move forward as a single, unified parish.

Accompaniment is not a practice that can be applied successfully on a piecemeal basis in a parish. If two members of the parish team are enthusiastic about an accompanying approach to discernment and formation but two others want to enforce the rules literally or adopt an "anything goes" approach, a pastoral and muddy mess results.

As the pastoral workers of a parish learn the art of accompaniment, the parish team—whether paid or unpaid—will want to work together in unity to embrace accompaniment as a pastoral strategy. Accompaniment thus becomes the "theme song" of parish life. The tone of everything that is said in public within the parish, from the homilies to the announcements to the structure of the programs, will echo it.

The process of decision making provides an opportunity to catechize the entire parish. When we open our doors to welcome people home, those members who never left may begin to feel like the "elder brother." Or there may be some among the existing regular parishioners who feel that accepting people back is taking mercy too far. We do need everyone to be part of the "welcoming committee," however, so accompanying the ones who are reluctant about this may also be part of your plan. In this regard, watch for the emergence of resentment where long-time leaders—lay, religious, or ordained—resent or resist letting "these sinners" back into the pews. Following our new norm, any person who resists in this way must always be treated with mercy and understanding. Accompany them to help them imagine and see what Jesus would want for this parish and for the ones finding their way home.

Making this decision as public as possible is part of the catechesis that is needed. Start discussing this in the bulletin, homilies, and announcements. Start building up hope that the church we dream of becoming—a parish of promise and hope—is on the horizon. Part of the catechesis in the parish is to teach that the Church is not a fortress to be guarded and protected from sinners. It's a tool of the Good Shepherd, a beacon of light to the world, and a place where people can find healing. In *The Joy of Love*, 291, we read this apt description:

> "The Church must accompany with attention and care the weakest of her children, who show signs of a wounded and troubled love, by restoring in them hope and confidence, like the beacon of a lighthouse in a port or a torch carried among the people to en-

lighten those who have lost their way or who are in the
midst of a storm." Let us not forget that the Church's
task is often like that of a field hospital.

And yes, *a beacon to the world* so that when the parishioners
themselves, the neighbors around the parish, or visitors see
this parish, they see the beacon. The torch we carry is the love
of Jesus and the mercy of God. Anyone who sees us should
see that love, forgiveness, and mercy.

Step 3. Plan together. Accompaniment is not accidental in
a parish. To succeed as a parish of accompaniment requires
that the pastor and parish team sit down together and do
some light planning. In many parishes today, this will mean
very little change. The pastoral team already has learned how
to accompany folks on their journeys of faith. Patience and
watchful love are already the stock and trade of everything
from the sacrament of reconciliation to faith-formation programs. Everyone is already welcomed to come in "just as they
are" but also encouraged to grow in faith.

Even in those parishes already doing the work of accompaniment, however, this effort can be enhanced by a small
amount of planning, a bit more training for everyone, and periodic parish evaluations based on the points of orientation
and guidelines for pastoral theology. All parishes benefit from
the parish-wide catechesis resulting from making a public decision to move forward as a parish of accompaniment.

A parish of accompaniment is one in which the pastor and
pastoral team intentionally portray a particular attitude and
posture toward all members of the parish, both the active as
well as the less active. The attitude is one of understanding

that no one is perfect. The posture is one of openness to the people who may struggle to follow the norms and policies of the Church. In an accompanying parish, the leaders recognize that people can only respond as they are able. They gradually grow toward the norms of the Church. The posture, therefore, is also one of acceptance, love, and patience.

As I said above, attitude really matters. If you tend to resent people or give up on them for being absent or breaking the rules, pay attention to that. If you tend to label people as unchurched or unfaithful, pay attention to that as well. If you're personally offended by latecomers to the reign of God after you've spent so many years following the Church more closely, remember that this is the way of Jesus. He wants all to come home and be within his saving reach. Remember the story he told of the vineyard owner who hired workers to harvest his crop. Some were there from daybreak, others from noon onward, and still others only in the final hours. But each was paid the same. Each was treated with the same, complete mercy. When challenged by the ones who had been present from the beginning, the owner asked simply, "Are you envious because I am generous?" (Matthew 20:1–16). In this parable, Jesus is teaching us how God behaves toward us even if we're latecomers and, therefore, how we should behave toward others no matter when they appear on our doorstep.

As parish leaders, let us pray that we will be filled with this same love and mercy. We desire to be like the father of the prodigal son. How we speak to those living outside our rules or beneath our norms is very important. Try to imagine what Jesus would say to them. Instead of judging or condemning, turn to them with compassion, mercy, and hope. Make sure your words are loving and kind.

Very little change of programs but a huge change of heart
The plan you prepare as a parish requires that you change very little about your existing programs, calendars, or team. The primary part of the plan will be to train and form everyone as an accompanist. Everyone? Yes, pretty much. This includes all parents to help them accompany their children. All spouses to accompany each other. Everyone to accompany the poor and wounded, the immigrant and the stranger. All the catechists to adopt an accompaniment model of religious education. All those working in liturgy to greatly expand how the weekend liturgies serve to accompany everyone, including those who don't feel welcome now. Everyone working in pastoral care—and their numbers will need to be increased—so their outreach in hospital, home, and neighborhood visits will more closely resemble the outreach of Jesus.

This training and formation can't happen all at once, of course, so the plan will describe how you will slowly but consistently bring everyone into the accompaniment circle. I remind you again of the words of the Holy Father in *The Joy of the Gospel*, 169, regarding this (italics mine):

> In our world, ordained ministers and other pastoral workers can make present the fragrance of Christ's closeness and his personal gaze. *The Church will have to initiate everyone*—priests, religious and laity—into this "art of accompaniment" which teaches us to remove our sandals before the sacred ground of the other (cf. Ex 3:5). The pace of this accompaniment must be steady and reassuring, reflecting our closeness and our compassionate gaze which also heals, liberates, and encourages growth in the Christian life.

So in sum, to get the art of accompaniment established as a real and working strategy within the existing ministries of a parish—education, pastoral care, liturgy, outreach, welcoming, and others—requires that parish leaders (1) study what this means in real terms, (2) take the time for a well-made and well-understood decision as a parish, and (3) plan ways to prepare and train people for this work. Accompaniment is the work of Jesus. It's how he approached the people to whom he ministered, and it's the style of ministry that allows us to "be Jesus" now for others. Let's consider how this would unfold in a given parish, ministry by ministry.

SECTION 4: PLANNING TO BE A PARISH OF ACCOMPANIMENT
Area 1: Liturgy

Nothing a parish does to provide for accompaniment is more important than what happens at Mass on the weekends. The most common way that people are in contact with and learn from the Church is through the Sunday liturgy.

Many experiences comprise the Sunday Mass, and it is a rich source of grace for those seeking to deepen their faith. The gathering itself teaches us that we are part of the people of God. Who could gather alone? It's a silly idea. Hence, in the arrival, greeting, and walk to the pew, people learn a great message every week. The liturgy of the Word is an important element in Catholic life. Week after week, we hear the Scriptures proclaimed and applied to our lives. Like a drumbeat in a marching band, this liturgical "cadence" rings in our spiritual ear. The often-repeated Eucharistic story unfolds in front of us each week as a spiritual drama in which God's love for us shines through. Even if we do not receive communion, standing among those who are in the family of God is vital. And finally, we are sent. And for what are we sent? To love and serve the Lord and one another. In itself, this is a vital catechetical message each week. We are sent to love and serve, and this is the basis for the discernment the seeker wishes to do.

As I said above, we know that many of the households registered in our parishes are not present at weekend liturgies—and who knows the reasons why? It might simply be that their faith grew cold. Or it might be that their marriage went on the rocks and they are either embarrassed or afraid to appear at Mass. It might be that they can't get to Mass because their spouse is not Catholic and there is resentment, pressure, or simply silence at home about faith.

Regardless of why they're absent, we believe that the inborn hunger for God that all humans experience is still there, operating in their lives. Christ still loves them and calls them home to himself. Within their own hearts, people know. Deep down, they know they want to be connected to the Church and their faith. But many of them simply do not feel welcome or don't know how to make their way back. Maybe they haven't come to Mass for a while or they feel they have some impediment that makes returning impossible. Yet they do want their kids to "get some religion." They do know how important gathering for worship is even if they can't make it part of their own lives at the moment.

One of the key features of parish accompaniment is to help make everyone who's in a situation like this—on the margins of the parish—feel welcome at the parish church and at Mass. It's necessary for the words of welcome to be warm, regular, and explicit. Remember here the story of Zacchaeus, which I treated at some length as an example of Jesus' style of ministry. The first step is a warm and hearty welcome. Because of this, every time we are in touch with the households of the parish, we should extend a genuine welcome to Mass.

Many parishes use the "Litany of Welcome" to both get the word out to those who don't know we love them and to catechize the rest of the parish about that. Many people never "hear their name" mentioned at Mass because they're on the lists of "outsiders." You can change that by offering an explicit welcome. Ask a parish leader to read this or a variation of it before Mass once a month or so. Or find a way to get the word out: whoever you are and whatever you've done, you belong to us because you belong to Christ!

THE LITANY OF WELCOME

Who are you? Are you divorced? Are you married with kids, worrying for them and committed to their welfare? Are you married for the second or even the third time? Are you a single parent struggling to make ends meet? Are you gay or lesbian? Well, if you are, then you belong to us because you belong to Christ. Christ is the host here today. Christ sets this table. And Christ welcomes all.

Are you lonely? Are you a widow? Are you a single man or woman who would prefer to have a spouse? Are you disabled or disfigured? Have you run out of luck? Are you living with shame? Have you been a prisoner? Well, if you are, then you belong to us because you belong to Christ. Christ is the host here today. Christ sets this table. And Christ welcomes all.

Are you a newcomer in this parish? An immigrant maybe? Are you from another Christian tradition? Are you full of doubt today, like Thomas? Has it been a while since you have come to this church? Or are you a regular here, full of faith and enthusiasm for the parish? Well, if you are, then you belong to us because you belong to Christ. Christ is the host here today. Christ sets this table. And Christ welcomes all.

All people of good will are welcome here: that's the really good news! If you've been away, you can come back. If you've been living in darkness, you can come to the light. If you haven't been able to believe without seeing him, look around you, the body of Christ has come to Mass today. Sinners are welcome. Saints, too. Everyone is welcome to come to Christ because we all belong to Christ. Christ is the host here today.

Don't worry that people who are invited and made to feel welcome will take advantage of your generosity. To be a parish of true promise and hope is to reflect the way of Jesus. Remember once again that we are sent to become the beacon on the hill, the light set on the lampstand illuminating the whole house. Jesus taught explicitly about this in Luke 14:

> [Jesus] said to the one who had invited him, "When you give a luncheon or a dinner, do not invite your friends or your brothers or your relatives or rich neighbors, in case they may invite you in return, and you would be repaid. But when you give a banquet, invite the poor, the crippled, the lame, and the blind. You

will be blessed because they cannot repay you for you
will be repaid at the resurrection of the righteous."

Likewise, at Sunday liturgy in an accompanying parish, a special word can be offered to non-Catholic spouses and friends to welcome them in Christ's name, make them feel at home, and help them learn how we celebrate the liturgy. But for all Catholics, whether in stable, approved marriages or not, whether single people, members of religious communities, or strangers dropping in on a spiritual search, the tone, tenor, and terminology used in the liturgy must be inclusive, respectful, and Christ-centered. Nothing we do at the parish is more important than this. We want everyone present to leave Mass feeling the force of grace that the liturgy offers to all.

How we address crowds of people who are present only at Christmas, Easter, funerals, and weddings is also very important. What is said in the homily can show that we love them as Jesus does. And likewise, how we speak to people in irregular situations in these and other settings is very important. These folks may not be able to hear their own conscience without accompaniment to help them. They may not know that they are forgiven or that they can gradually move toward God again in their lives. We may be their bridge to that, and our compassionate words are the key.

Area 2: Reconciliation

For many people, the journey back to the heart of the Church will eventually include the sacrament of reconciliation. Remember the steps outlined in Part 2 that Bishop McElroy articulated for us, the ones that Jesus followed with Zacchaeus:

- First, we embrace each person without judgment, even if the culture of the society or Church judges them harshly.
- Second, we love them and allow them to tell their story, which is the step usually known as the confession. As we move more and more into accompaniment, presiders in reconciliation may invite people to tell their whole story rather than recite a list of sins. This will help the penitent discern areas where growth is possible.
- Third, we help them discern the voice of the Lord as he seeks them out and saves them. This discernment is the key to accompaniment.

In this sacrament, of course, there is a rite to follow, and certain steps are required for both the penitent and the presider. In all of these steps and moments, however, mercy and compassion must be foremost. This sacrament—the actions, words, and gestures—is vital for those on the road to holiness. The grace of reconciliation is a powerful aid in the Christian life.

Communal celebrations of the sacrament of reconciliation are also an option in most places. For those who have been away from the sacrament for a length of time and are making their way back only gradually, the communal context may be a needed stepping stone.

In the tradition of the Church, God's mercy is at the heart of this sacrament. One's sins are likewise forgiven in the opening penitential act of the Mass and each time we sing the Gloria or the Lamb of God ("You take away the sins of the world, have mercy on us"). Whenever we give alms or help a person in need or reach out in forgiveness to a sister or brother, our own sins are forgiven: "Forgive us our sins as we forgive those who sin against us."

Internal forum

For those who are currently living in second marriages in cases where the first marriage has not been officially annulled, *The Joy of Love* proposes an examen in article 300. Then it says this, in part:

> What we are speaking of is a process of accompaniment and discernment which "guides the faithful to an awareness of their situation before God. Conversation with the priest, in the internal forum, contributes to the formation of a correct judgment on what hinders the possibility of a fuller participation in the life of the Church and on what steps can foster it and make it grow. Given that gradualness is not in the law itself (cf. *Familiaris Consortio*, 34), this discernment can never prescind from the Gospel demands of truth and charity, as proposed by the Church. For this discernment to happen, the following conditions must necessarily be present: humility, discretion and love for the Church and her teaching, in a sincere search for God's will and a desire to make a more perfect response to it." (The quote within this section is taken from the final *relatio* of the 2015 synod #85.)

Hence, in the sacrament of reconciliation, when there is adequate time and even multiple visits between the priest and the one seeking to be healed, and when the attitudes expressed just above are met, it is possible that one can reach a point in discernment of certainty about what God himself is asking of this person in this particular situation.

Area 3: Pastoral care and outreach

In a parish of mercy and accompaniment, the pastoral care and outreach work may become one of the most vital ways in which accompaniment occurs. Leaders learn how to insert practices of mercy into pastoral care and outreach ministries, including to non-Catholic spouses and partners.

Pastoral care ministers may offer the sick and dying special mercy and accompaniment to achieve healing or a peaceful death in Christ. They may seek out the inactive members of the parish one-by-one to say once again to them, "We are the people of God, and you are part of our family. We welcome you regardless of your situation in life." These absent ones, as I said above, may very well be living lives of sacrifice and love, even if not within the norm of the official Church. Care should be taken not to judge them as somehow absent from God. By listening to them, we may learn a great deal about why they no longer worship with the parish.

We must be careful not to jump to conclusions—let's not assume the second marriage is adultery. It may very well not be if there are mitigating circumstances. Let's not reduce that same-sex couple to sexual acts. Their lives are much richer and more holy than that. Instead, listen to the whole story, offering hope and comfort. Help them discern the voice of God in their conscience. Let's not assume that the couple living together without marriage is somehow unreachable. There may well be a lot of love and self-giving in that household. Holiness doesn't occur only in perfect homes.

When they are ready, guide that remarried couple to the

tribunal, if needed and appropriate. Challenge all couples to let go of promiscuity, lust, and pornography. Encourage them to become active in parish life. Introduce them to others who share their journey. This means we must avoid black-and-white thinking about people. We are all God's children.

Likewise, the poor of our neighborhoods, nation, and world. To these we have been given a special calling since whatever we do for them, we do for Christ himself.

> This entails appreciating the poor in their goodness, in their experience of life, in their culture, and in their ways of living the faith....The poor person, when loved, "is esteemed as of great value...." Only based on this real and sincere closeness can we properly accompany the poor on their path of liberation. Only this will ensure that "in every Christian community, the poor feel at home." *The Joy of the Gospel*, 199

Send people home

The pastoral care team might work together to plan ways to reach out to people who have, in the past, felt alienated from the Church. One powerful way to do this is to equip the active members of the parish to speak to their own children and family, to their neighbors and friends, and assure them that our attitude and posture toward them has changed. To tell them that our hearts are open to them. We are ready to accompany them without first condemning them. Teach your active members how to invite and welcome people in God's name. Catholics are often hesitant to speak about their faith to others. They don't want to appear to proselytize or offer unsolicited evangelical advice to people.

But of course, welcoming people and sharing one's faith is precisely what we want everyone to do. This describes the "spirit-filled evangelizers" that Pope Francis dreams of for the Church.[43] With a small bit of preparation, Catholics can indeed become more ready to do this without annoying their friends and family.[44] The first thing we want our parishioners to do is to live their Christian lives authentically and then to speak about how much they treasure their faith, how important it is to share the liturgy every weekend, and how the renewed Church wants everyone to return and be included. This authenticity becomes a credential when they want to speak of faith to someone else.

However, a parish can only send people home to invite others to return to the parish if indeed the parish is ready and willing to take them in without judgment and with mercy. This must become part of the plan, but it may not be the first step. Inviting family members to speak to each other is important because no one can reach out to others like those who know them well. In speaking of the mission of the parish, Pope Francis describes it like this in *The Joy of the Gospel*, 28:

> This presumes that [the parish] really is in contact with the homes and the lives of its people, and does not become a useless structure out of touch with people or a self-absorbed group made up of a chosen few. The parish is the presence of the Church in a given territory, an environment for hearing God's word, for growth in the Christian life, for dialogue, proclamation, charitable outreach, worship and celebration. In all its activities the parish encourages and trains its members to [invite and welcome others in God's name]. It is

a community of communities, a sanctuary where the
thirsty come to drink in the midst of their journey, and
a center of constant missionary outreach.

Area 4: Religious education

In an accompanying parish, we learn how to accompany each
family that is part of the religious education program. As I just
observed, many of these families are not at Mass on the weekend, but we continue to reach out to them, to invite them to
participate more fully, and to show them our love. Many families struggle to keep up with all the various deadlines, rules,
and requirements of the parish program. To the leaders, these
all seem reasonable and necessary, but to many families, they
are quite difficult. In particular, single-parent homes and ecumenical families—where only one parent is juggling compet-
ing demands—can find our deadlines difficult to meet. For
the leaders, this means special sacrifices are needed: we have
to give up our rigidity and become more flexible.

In all we do in religious education, our model for accompaniment is the remarkable role that sponsors play in the
RCIA. The catechumenate is an ancient institution in the
Church. From the beginning, Church leaders believed that it
was essential for everyone moving deeper into the faith to be
supported and accompanied by another Christian. Today, in
our discussion of accompaniment in the parish, we are saying
no less.

Sacrament preparation: Parents first. Hence, every child
should have a parent accompanist. Every parent should have
access to a pastoral accompanist at the parish.

We know that most active adult Catholics today are with

the Church because they were formed in faith by their parents or guardians. Of course, some people do come to faith as adults, but for the majority, the key element is formation by their parents when they were children.

And in forming children, parents are more essential than religious education programs. No matter how well we may do in religious education classes with that eight-year-old child, if he or she goes home to a house where the faith is not cherished or understood, our best efforts can't produce formation that will last a lifetime. The parents—by their actions, words, and household habits—form their children for life, either with faith or without it. What if we commissioned parents to form the faith of their own kids?

It will never be enough, however, for catechetical leaders to simply hand the parents a textbook, send them home, and wish them luck. Instead, it's necessary to accompany these young parents to help them form their own children using a resource designed for this purpose. Accompaniment means that we literally stand by their side and help them to be successful.[45] They might not have all the terminology just right. They might not be totally enthused in their own faith. They might not even be worshiping with the Church regularly. But once they begin to form their own children, and we coach them to do this well, they quickly become more confident, more informed, and more prayerful.

It turns out that when we coach young parents at the time of their children's first celebration of the sacraments, many find a new priority in living their own faith as examples for their children. They see themselves as role models and begin taking a more active role in the parish, including more regular attendance at Sunday Mass. By coaching and accompanying them to help their children, we wind up evangelizing the parishioners who are in their twenties and thirties.

Personal accompaniment chats. One of the essential keys to success in helping parents form their children at the time of the first sacraments is something we do for the parents alone. Parishes who work with accompaniment invite each set of parents—or the single parent if that's the case—to a brief chat as part of the preparation period for baptism, reconciliation, Eucharist, confirmation, or any other key moment. When there are two parents, both should be invited regardless of whether or not the marriage is valid, both are Catholic, they're cohabiting, or they're in a same-sex relationship. As part of the program, it's important to make it widely known that these interview chats are part and parcel of what everyone does. No one is being singled out. No one is being treated any differently than anyone else.

In keeping with the personalist guideline, the invitation should be both in writing and via the phone. Set a mutually handy time, allowing the parents to decide this according to their availability. This requires generous flexibility on the part of the parish accompanist. In the written invitation, make known the purpose. The purpose is not to pass along program information, dates, or other details. It is also not to "test" the parents about their faith or their activity in the parish. The positive purpose is twofold: (1) to set the stage for their child's experience of the sacrament and (2) to invite the parents to "tell their story of faith," their spiritual biography if you will, so that the parish can offer any assistance that might be helpful.

The person making this invitation and hosting this chat— the accompanist—could be a trained volunteer or a paid team member. Normally, the accompanist needs to set aside about forty-five minutes per family. The host accompanist begins simply by making them feel welcome—and many will not be comfortable at first. A little small talk here goes a long way, especially for families who have never before had a serious conversation with anyone at the parish. The room in which this chat is held should be quiet, private, warmly lighted, and intimate. Refreshments are a huge help—coffee, tea, sodas, water, and a bite to eat.

— ILLUSTRATION —

St. Mary's Parish and Richard, the catechetical leader

Let me introduce you to St. Mary's Parish and Richard, the parish catechetical leader. St. Mary's has a first communion class of eighty-seven, so when Rich first considered interviewing each set of parents in the preparation period, he was very doubtful it would work. He thought the number of parents would be too large, but he is committed to accompaniment as a strategy, seeing it as a valuable way to get beneath the surface of people's lives to the deeper issues. So he put out the word in the fall that he would need a dozen volunteers for this task. He was hoping to find slightly older members of the parish, and that's exactly who he recruited. As soon as he had enough volunteers, he scheduled a training day.

"People of a certain age have two qualities that make this work," he reported later. "First, they are naturally grandparent-like and approachable. Second, they've heard everything, so nothing shocks them." Rich found that his accompaniment team was easy to assemble for training (more on the training later), which he did several weeks before the beginning of the preparation program for first reconciliation. Each family would be scheduled for one chat, even though two sacraments were being celebrated in the year.

Monica, one of the trained accompanists, was sixty-eight years old, retired from nursing, and the mom of three grown children. She had been attending periodic sessions on spiritual companionship at a local Catholic women's college, and in the past year had joined the Taizé prayer group at that college. The accompaniment training occurred on a Saturday in early October (first reconciliation was planned for the Advent season), and seven volunteers took part. Monica found the sharing around the group to be very helpful to her own spirituality and felt that the training answered all her concerns and questions. She felt ready to go; she was ready to meet her first family.

Rich decided it would be best for all accompaniment chats to occur at the parish offices. There were issues of safety and security involved, but also, as the catechetical leader, Rich wanted to shake some hands, be in the wings, and be available if ever needed. The catechetical team converted some small rooms into comfortable sitting areas. They used donated lamps and furniture from charity shops. The staff coffee area provided the source for refreshments. At first, they thought two spaces would be enough, but it turned out that many parents wanted to schedule their chats at similar times, so they created four spaces. These came to be known as "accompaniment rooms" and were frequently scheduled by other team members in the parish as well. They named their rooms

Emmaus, Zacchaeus, Jairus, and Mary of Bethany, four examples of accompaniment from the life of Jesus.

One issue that Rich did not foresee was providing babysitting for young couples so both of them could attend the chat.
In the first reconciliation and communion preparation program, this parish asked the parents to be present for each of
six sessions for each sacrament and to teach the lesson to their
own child. Childcare had also been an issue for these sessions,
and the parish had decided not to provide any babysitting on
the parish campus due to the need to provide for the protec-
tion of minors. Instead, they asked the sodalities of the parish
to raise funds to pay for the regular babysitters the couple
would use for other reasons. Families that could not afford
frequent babysitters made use of the fund. This childcare fund
had enough in it to also support the accompaniment chats.

Back to Monica. After several phone calls back and forth
to find a date for a meeting, Trevor and Crystal appeared one
Thursday evening about 5:30. It was clear that Trevor had got-
ten home from work only a short time before this and picked
up Crystal, and they arrived at the parish slightly out of breath
and hurried. To Monica, they looked very young, but they were
both in their late twenties. Josh was the first of their two children to prepare for the sacraments. His sister, Emma, was two
years behind him. Monica set them and herself up with sodas
and a small plate of cheese and crackers she had prepared.

The chat itself began with a conversation about the weather.
The autumn had been especially warm that year, and Monica
started there. Second up in the conversation was the World
Series, which would begin shortly. The local team was doing
quite well. She asked about their jobs, their extended families,
and their children. As she had been trained to do, Monica did

not take notes or appear to be any sort of therapist.

Finally, after the small talk wound down, Monica turned to her first piece of business, which she had been trained to keep very brief. She made a statement in her own words saying that this parish welcomes everyone and walks with each family, regardless of their situations. She told them that the parish places no particular demand on them as a family but simply keeps open the door to whatever the family is ready to do at the parish. Crystal responded, saying she had been hearing the priest say something like this at Mass from time to time, and she was grateful they weren't being pushed too fast. "Trevor was raised Lutheran and wasn't very comfortable with the whole Catholic thing," she told Monica. He had agreed to come with her to the sacrament preparation nights, and Monica could see this was important to Crystal. Trevor was mainly silent.

Monica then shifted gears and invited them to tell their stories. "Tell me about your own faith journey. What was your family's background with churchy stuff?" she asked. "Were your parents in a church? Did you celebrate the holidays?" Crystal gave her a wide-eyed look and said, "No one's ever asked us about that." But then she told the story of her parents: Catholic mom, a dad who never went to church at all. Three siblings, all left the Church. Christmas was usually with the grandparents. Dad had died four years earlier, but the funeral was at the cemetery chapel because the priest at the time refused to have it at the parish where they lived. They'd delayed the baptism of Josh until his sister was born. "We weren't really sure," she said, "whether to be Catholic or not."

"How did you make up your mind?" Monica asked.

"Well, you know, in the back of your mind, you sorta know what you have to do," she said. "It's what's right for the kids."

"How about you, Trevor?" Monica asked. "Oh, it's not a good story," he told her. Parents divorced. Dad drunk a lot. Moved to a trailer park with a girlfriend. Mom is just forty-eight now, so she was young when he was born. She remarried about ten years ago but the new husband is great. Belongs to a Lutheran church but rarely attends services. "My first happy Christmas was with Crystal's family," he said, and then he reached for her hand but pulled back.

"It's OK," Monica motioned. He reached out again. It was the first sign of affection Monica had noticed between them, but they were gradually becoming more comfortable. A lot of people in love never touch each other when they're at their local church, Monica told me later. It's like, you can't do that here, or something, she said.

"She'd like me to turn Catholic," Trevor added, looking over at Crystal. Monica gave Crystal the floor.

"Well, he's already sorta Catholic," Crystal said. "He comes with me on Sundays sometimes, not that I'm here every week or anything. Well, I mean, I'm here pretty often. When I can." Crystal had talked herself into a bit of a corner, but Monica let her out of it.

"What do you think, Trevor?"

"To be honest, I don't know," he said. "There are some things I hear from the Church, like about gays or birth control, and I think, 'They're way out of date.' Two of our best friends are a gay couple. Great guys. But I don't know. I'm thinking it over."

"Well, when you're ready to talk more about that, give me a call," Monica said. They continued chatting for another half an hour and Monica reported later that she could feel that they had made a good connection. Then they slowly wound down their chat, said their goodbyes, and parted. Monica got an email from Crystal the next day thanking her profusely for the chat. "I think you opened a door," she said. "He's never talked about any of this before."

Evaluation from Monica's point of view
Monica and Richard sat down to evaluate this session a few days later. Because there was nothing to report (such as abuse of some kind), and to keep confidential what she had heard,[46] Monica left out most of the content of her chat while talking with Rich. She mainly shared about "her performance" in the session and how she felt she handled things. She felt she had followed the guidelines for accompaniment rather well: making herself available when they were free, keeping mercy and compassion uppermost in her mind, letting them talk, withholding her own judgments, seeing their various mitigating circumstances, letting gradualism unfold (for example, in his decision whether or not to become Catholic), being a servant to them, and so forth.

What had surprised Monica was that telling their stories was all they needed for various personal and religious matters to open up. She fully expected to see them again, even though this was their only "required" accompaniment chat. (She did see them again, by the way. Trevor was received into full communion at the Easter Vigil a year later.)

Evaluation from Rich's point of view
For Rich, the work of organizing these chats, preparing the accompaniment rooms, and training the accompanists really paid off. The formation of the children in the preparation process moved forward with much more energy. The parents

were no longer strangers at the parish as some of them had been for a long time. Other ministries in the parish began using chats like these to allow people to tell their stories and move forward. And most of all, many families were restored to being more present at the weekend liturgies because they were personally invited.

Rich also reported that he heard from the parents. Over and over again they told him that as long as they could remember, no one at the parish had ever actually talked and listened to them. No one had asked about their families, their stories, and their situations. A large number of parents shared very personal information, assured they would not be judged harshly for it. In a way, those accompaniment rooms became the heart of the ministry to parents, which was gradually becoming the mission of the catechetical program for Rich.

"Two years ago," he told me, "we would definitely have said that our mission is to the children. It was to provide them with religious education and the sacraments. But now we see that our ministry is actually to their parents, first and foremost. It's to equip them to form their children, but also to provide them with a safe place in the Church to explore their own faith and to have us accompany them. So many personal situations, past mistakes, bad choices, or downright selfish behavior came out in those accompaniment rooms," he told me. "They're like the new confessionals."

Finally, Rich and his team of accompanists reached a decision early in the process that each accompanist should be paid a small stipend for their time and effort. The payment is $12 per session. For the accompanists, it was a matter of justice. Accompaniment is a regular, recurring ministry now and a strong element of many programs in the parish.

Furthermore, it requires that the accompanists be available mainly on weekends and evenings when most parishioners are free. Rich also felt they should be paid because it allows him to call them to greater accountability. It provides him with a designated team, one steeped in the skills needed for accompaniment, one that he can continue to train and form, and one that he can promise will be professional and confidential about everything they hear and see.

Let me pause here to commiserate with fellow parish ministers. This change of pace for us from replacing parents with catechists to helping parents form their own children in the faith—with our accompaniment—is a real and difficult challenge. But we know it is the future for the Church. We can do this. We can accompany parents and offer them assurance and affirmation.

After the first sacraments

The accompaniment model for faith formation and religious education applies to every age and every stage of catechetical ministry. After the first sacraments have been celebrated is a good time to plan for the following year of accompaniment for those parents. Even if catechists conduct the weekly classes—although it's best if you continue to maintain a role for the parents instead—you can build in annual accompaniment chats and other moments of contact with the parents. This adds a rich layer to the program. In the second year of chats, the parents are no longer new to this. In the year after the first sacraments, rather than inquiring about family history and background, you might inquire about any questions they may have, any concerns, or any ways in which they might become more involved.

Again, the single most important idea in all of this is that unless the parents of our children are deeply and fully involved in both the formal education and a daily lifestyle of faith, we cannot succeed with their children. This is one of our greatest challenges. Accompaniment of parents becomes the way forward.

As long as we keep "doing it for them," parents will never step up and become the persons primarily responsible for the faith of their children. We are in the habit of replacing parents with parish volunteers for this purpose. The volunteers are well-meaning and faithful. They want to succeed with the children. But, by continually replacing parents with catechists or teachers at the parish, we have unfortunately taught the parents that their role is minor. In fact, though, their role is irreplaceable. Here's what the document on Christian education from Vatican II said about that:

> The role of parents in education is of such importance that it is almost impossible to provide an adequate substitute. DECLARATION ON CHRISTIAN EDUCATION, 3

Baptism prep and post-baptism care

I began the discussion of the accompaniment model for religious education with sacrament preparation for reconciliation and first communion, but the same principles and practices apply at the time of baptism. In most parishes, there are two groups of young couples or single parents who are bringing their children for baptism. One group is in the class of families in the Church today where the faith does continue to be passed from generation to generation. They actually do have God-talk and other faith elements of many kinds in their homes. They are frequent participants in the life of the parish, and their child or children will certainly be present with them at those times.

The other group (which is larger) is only marginally involved in parish life. They appear at our doorstep mainly when need drives them to us: birth, death, marriage, crises of various kinds, or the holidays.

Both of these groups of young parents benefit from the accompaniment model[47] for baptism preparation. The topics in the accompaniment chats associated with baptism prep, like those for first reconciliation or first communion, are not about the details of the sacrament, the schedule for the rite, or other such matters. They're a time to invite the young parents to reflect on having this new person around the house. In these chats, it's perfectly fine and desirable that they bring the infant or young child with them to the chat. It's also a time to celebrate this birth. What could be more important?

What happens "after the plunge" and the baptism is over? Keeping in touch and continuing to accompany families during those early years is vital. Again, the accompaniment model[48] provides tools and suggestions for continuing to be present to each family.

Confirmation prep

Likewise, confirmation preparation is an opportunity to help young people, their sponsors, and their parents renew their faith as adults. As in all of faith formation in the elementary years, what role do we offer to parents? How do we accompany parents to play their role? How do we coach young parents who may not have anyone else as a model of faith? How do we help them become the primary teachers of their own children?

If confirmation is being offered to young adults in their teens, the accompaniment model[49] works perfectly and allows you to have a "chat" with each candidate as well as with each set of parents.

Area 5: Marriage preparation

The period of preparation for marriage is a very busy one in every couple's life. They're planning a huge party to which they will invite nearly everyone they've ever met. But it is possible in the marriage preparation process to create a relationship that doesn't end at the wedding. Listening to young couples and their concerns is a way for the parish to learn about their needs. It requires that we listen to them carefully. All marriage prep should be designed as a process of accompaniment in which we help them discern God's voice. In the first place, this means that we accompany each couple instead of working with couples in large groups. In the second place, it requires that couples have or develop a fundamental orientation toward the Holy. Pope Francis has made some suggestions about this in *The Joy of Love*, especially in articles 205 and onward:

> There are a number of legitimate ways to structure programs of marriage preparation, and each local Church will discern how best to provide a suitable formation without distancing young people from the sacrament. They do not need to be taught the entire *Catechism* or overwhelmed with too much information. Here too, "it is not great knowledge, but rather the ability to feel and relish things interiorly that contents and satisfies the soul." ARTICLE 207

At this point in a couple's life, organizing to provide for a series of chats with an accompanist is very effective and might be done "couple to couple." Many times, the couple is not ready to disclose in a group setting many of the issues they may face. Each of them has a history, and that history often includes poor choices, mistakes, and selfish behaviors they now regret but that form the history on which their future life as a couple will be built. When you as a pastoral accompanist invite them to tell their story, and they can do so without judgment or preaching, marvelous healing can come from it. You strengthen the coming marriage with your efforts.

Area 6: Conversion opportunities at the parish

How the parish programs are organized to assist parishioners in the turning of the heart also determines whether you're an accompanying parish or not. As I said above, in the very first words he addressed to the Church in article 3 and onward of *The Joy of the Gospel*, Pope Francis invites everyone to turn his or her heart to Christ. Jesus will not disappoint anyone who does that, he promised. This turning of the heart is how folks encounter Christ. And this encounter is the basis of all accompaniment. Friendship with Jesus is the hallmark of Christian and Catholic life. Parishes that are committed to accompaniment must find ways to help the many members who have never experienced conversion or who have not had their initial encounter with Jesus.

There are existing tools to assist you, such as the parish-based retreat known as *The Sanctus Retreat*[50] and resources for faith sharing at parish meetings. Bishop Ray Lucker instructed his diocesan team in New Ulm, Minnesota, in the 1980s to make sure that opportunities for faith sharing were built into the plan for every parish meeting in that diocese. Such regular faith sharing continually leads people to the turning of the heart.

In a sense, everything in the parish is an opportunity for spiritual growth, and one might see a pastoral accompanist for any of the reasons and at any of the moment in life I mentioned above. In pastoral theology, the goal is to make an accompanist available to anyone in the parish who seeks one. One's reason for sitting down with an accompanist may be (1) to explore how to maintain a closer relationship with Jesus, how to turn one's heart to him right smack in the middle of everyday life. (2) Or it may be to make a good decision or to embrace changes in one's life. (3) Or possibly simply to share one's hopes, struggles, or losses. (4) It may be to grow as a Christian, embracing more deeply the call to love the poor, care for the earth, or work for justice.

Learning the skills of accompaniment

Parishes that are moving toward accompaniment are filled with new energy and excitement as people sense the potential in offering people the promise of mercy and the hope of being welcome. The training needed to prepare accompanists for their new ministry in the parish is not extensive, but it is essential. It can be done in a one-day seminar offered right at the parish. In the seminar, potential accompanists are offered a chance to deepen their experience of the Paschal Mystery, to learn how to follow the points of orientation in pastoral ministry, and to follow the guidelines for accompaniment as I outlined them in this text. They are schooled in listening skills and using theological reflection; the skills and process of accompaniment; church teaching; dealing with situations that require reporting (abuse, violence, etc.); when to call in the parish priest, send a matter to the tribunal, or make use of professional counselors; confidentiality; working as a team by evaluating and supporting each other within the parish; and the skills of discernment.

A second level of preparation is aimed at the whole parish. As the "voice of the parish" becomes one of compassion and mercy, and as the parish slowly opens wide its doors to people, we want our active parishioners to become our ambassadors. We will prepare everyone to speak about their faith and attend to the life situations of the ones closest to them—spouses, children, the wider family, neighbors, and friends. Such parish-wide preparation is delivered through existing programs and does not require that everyone take part in extensive training days.

APPENDIX

I. POINTS OF ORIENTATION FOR PASTORAL THEOLOGY
Encounter with the person of Jesus Christ
1. This is our first point of orientation. Pastoral theology turns and pivots on the presence and grace of Jesus Christ in all we teach and do. Therefore, when we enact pastoral ministry, we do so under the power of grace with Jesus acting through us. He is the power or energy that holds everything together (Colossians 1:15). We are forgiven and loved unconditionally by Jesus.

Sinners leading sinners
2. Our second point of orientation in pastoral theology is that we who enact pastoral ministry are forgiven and loved un-conditionally by Jesus. We are sinners leading other sinners to the Lord. The profound reality of being forgiven may be the most difficult element of our faith to believe. Since we are forgiven, in whose name would we ever withhold mercy from someone else?

A personalist theology

3. Our third point of orientation is that pastoral theology is personalist. The encounter with Jesus is always a person-to-person experience. Each person is on a unique journey of faith. For this reason, we do not apply the law of the Church to everyone equally, for example, but we consider each case in light of the individual's conscience.

Liturgy as source and summit

4. The fourth point of orientation in pastoral theology is the liturgy of the Church, where we gather together in love and solidarity. This is where Jesus comes to stand among us as friend and comforter. It's "the source and summit of our lives" (*The Constitution on the Liturgy*, 10). For this reason, all the faithful are called to full, active, and conscious participation in the liturgy each week (*Liturgy*, 11).

The Paschal Mystery

5. The fifth point of orientation in pastoral theology is the Paschal Mystery, which calls us to find meaning in suffering by listening for the divine call embedded in our human experiences and situations. Entering into this dying and rising helps us know that we are children of God (Romans 8:16).

God is still speaking

6. Pastoral theology takes its lead from the fact that God is still speaking to us. It is amazing and remarkable, but God, yes, the creator of the world, Jesus the Lord, and the Holy Spirit, is communicating God's self to each of us, and through discernment, we can hear the voice of God in our lives. Every single day.

Grace

7. Grace is a free gift from a loving God. It is offered to each person along with the freedom to accept or reject it. Grace empowers or guides us to be all that we're created, forgiven, saved, and loved to become.

II. GUIDELINES FOR OPERATING THE PARISH OF ACCOMPANIMENT

Offering radical availability

1. Priests or other pastoral workers offer radical availability to people seeking accompaniment.

Always acting with mercy

2. Pastoral ministry is a work of mercy, especially toward those most in need of our love and compassion. We ask ourselves, "What would Jesus say or do in this situation with this particular person?"

Understanding mitigating circumstances

3. The mercy of which we're speaking here leads us in pastoral theology to pay attention to the mitigating circumstances in people's lives.

Putting people before law

4. Pastoral theology always puts "people first." First before canon law and first before the machinery of church courts and propositional doctrine.

Learning patience and gradualism

5. Gradualism is the long-taught idea that people grow into intimacy with Christ and become able to follow the way of the Church gradually.

Employing a gentle, sacred inquiry

6. Inasmuch as accompaniment helps people "read" or "interpret" the gospel in light of their situations, experiences, questions, or decisions, pastoral theology is a hermeneutical activity. For purposes of pastoral theology in the parish, we will call this activity by the name of a "sacred inquiry."

Making restoration and integration happen

7. Pastoral theology has the goal of helping to integrate and restore people to full life in the Church.

Learning the art of accompaniment

8. The methodology for enacting pastoral theology is authentic accompaniment in which we respect and honor the marvelous and mysterious work of God in people's lives. Accompaniment of this sort unfolds in God's time, encouraged and observed with patience and love.

Dealing with the power of darkness

9. Pastoral theology occurs in a forum where the power of darkness is constantly striving to be divisive, dishonest, and hateful.

Practicing servant ministry

10. In pastoral theology, the minister is the servant to the community. There are no seats of privilege in pastoral ministry.

Allowing for the primacy of one's conscience

11. The outcome of pastoral ministry is to help people discern the voice of God echoing in the depths of each one's conscience. The pastoral Church is a nonjudgmental Church.

Answering the call to holiness

12. If the context for pastoral ministry is the Church and if the Church is composed of the people of God who are both the enactors and receivers of pastoral ministry, then the hallmark of the people of God and the goal of all pastoral ministry is the journey to holiness.

ENDNOTES

1. Thomas Groome and Robert Imbelli, "Signposts towards a Pastoral Theology," *Theological Studies* 53, 1992.

2. "Interview with Gustavo Gutiérrez," *Maryknoll Magazine* 80 (November 1986) 19, quoted by Groom and Imbelli.

3. By Antonio Spadaro, SJ, editor of *La Civiltà Cattolica*, "A Big Heart Open to God: An Interview with Pope Francis." Published in *America* Magazine, September 30, 2013.

4. "'I Am a Sinner': The Deep Humility of Pope Francis." Stephen Bullivant, *America* Magazine, September 25, 2013.

5. "*Misericordia et misera* is a phrase used by Saint Augustine in recounting the story of Jesus' meeting with the woman taken in adultery (cf. Jn 8:1–11). It would be difficult to imagine a more beautiful or apt way of expressing the mystery of God's love when it touches the sinner: 'the two of them alone remained: *mercy with misery*'" (from the opening of the document).

6. *Misericordia et misera*, 1.

7. David Haas. "Now We Remain" (Chicago: GIA Publications, Inc).

8. From the *National Catholic Reporter*, May 25, 2001.

9. Ernesto Balducci, *John: The Transitional Pope*, trans. Dorothy White (New York: McGraw-Hill, 1965).

10. Spadaro, see note 3.

11. Blase J. Cupich. *America* Magazine, December 29, 2017.

12. "Anyone who divorces his wife, except on the ground of unchastity, causes her to commit adultery; and whoever marries a divorced woman commits adultery."

13. Marriage as covenant was defined at Vatican II, replacing the old "legal contract" language of the 1917 Code of Canon Law. The revised Code says this in canon 1055 (which is the theological canon that defines marriage as it is to be understood in the Latin Church): "The marriage covenant, by which a man and a woman establish between themselves a partnership of their whole life, and which of its own very nature is ordered to the well-being of the spouses and to the procreation and upbringing of children, has, between the baptized, been raised by Christ the Lord to the dignity of a sacrament."

14. William P. Roberts in chapter 12, "Christian Marriage" in Raymond F. Bulman and Frederick J. Parrella, *From Trent to Vatican II: Historical and Theological Investigations* (Oxford University Press, 2006), 220–22.

15. *Catechism of the Catholic Church*, 1776.

16. Bishop Robert McElroy in a speech delivered at the 2018 assembly of the Association of U.S. Catholic Priests in June 2018, Albuquerque, NM.

17. McElroy, see note 16.

18. Drew Christiansen, SJ: "A Pastor to His People," *America*, April 8, 2016.

19. Spadaro, see note 3.

20. Apostolic Exhortation *Familiaris Consortio* (November 22, 1981), 34.

21. Michael Kirwin, SJ, "Reading the Signs of the Times" (in *Keeping Faith in Practice: Aspects of Catholic Pastoral Theology* [London: SCM Press, 2010]). I am indebted to Kirwin for his incisive treatment of hermeneutics as they relate to pastoral theology. He reminds us that, as precisely as one might develop a hermeneutic or method for interpretation of today's signs of the times, there always remains a dose of doubt and ambiguity in the outcome of the interpretation.

22. The term "hermeneutic" is not a pastoral word. It is Greek in origin and would be translated into Latin as *interpretare*, meaning how we interpret or find the discoverable meaning in what we read, hear, and see. It's close to the word we use to describe how we study Scripture: exegesis. It's an effort to understand written or verbal communication. In pastoral theology we prefer to use the term "sacred inquiry," which is a way to help

someone peer into the mystery of their experience to interpret it in the light of the Gospel. In the *Constitution on the Church in the Modern World* we find a mandate to interpret the signs of the times in this same light, requiring that we develop and test a hermeneutic to do that.

23. Martin B. Copenhaver, *Jesus Is the Question: The 307 Questions Jesus Asked and the 3 He Answered* (Abingdon Press, September 2, 2014).

24. McElroy, see note 16.

25. McElroy, see note 16.

26. See Catherine Clifford, "Pope Francis' Call for the Conversion of the Church in our Time" (Australian eJournal of Theology, April 2015).

27. Bernard Lonergan, SJ, *Method in Theology* (New York: Seabury, 1972).

28. Thomas Groome, *Sharing Faith* (San Francisco: Harper, 1991).

29. John Shea, *Alternative Futures for Worship*, ed. M. Cowan (Collegeville, MN: Liturgical Press, 1987).

30. Joe Holland and Peter Henriot, SJ, *Social Analysis: Linking Faith and Justice* (Washington, DC: Orbis Books, 1984).

31. Stephen Bevans, *Models of Contextual Theology* (Maryknoll, NY: Orbis Books, 2002).

32. James D. and Evelyn Eaton Whitehead, *Method in Ministry* (New York: Sheed and Ward, 1995).

33. Patricia O'Connell Killen and John de Beer, *The Art of Theological Reflection* (New York: Crossroad, 1995).

34. From the opening speech of St. John XXIII at Vatican II, paraphrased slightly.

35. Article 231 and following in *The Joy of the Gospel*.

36. One such text that presents the entire *Catechism* in either plain English or Spanish is *Our Catholic Life* (New London, CT: Twenty-Third Publications, 2017). This resource also has an *Imprimatur*.

37. Vatican City, September 4, 2015 (CNA/EWTN News)

38. For more on this, see Robert J. Schreiter, *Constructing Local Theologies* (Maryknoll, NY: Orbis Books, 1985).

39. For more on this, see Wright's material sponsored by Loyola Press at https://www.ignatianspirituality.com/25557/consolation-and-desolation-2.

40. "What Is Theological Reflection?" A guide from the Rev. Dr. Richard Dickey, 6/2006.

41. This is from *Our Catholic Faith* (Twenty-Third Publications, 2018). This is a study guide and summary of the entire *Catechism* but written in plain English. The section on suicide in the *Catechism* runs from articles 2280–2283. This is also available in Spanish.

42. Clifford, see note 26.

43. Chapter 5 of *The Joy of the Gospel.*

44. Credit goes to Martin Pable, OFM Cap, *Reclaim the Fire: A Parish Guide to Evangelization* (ACTA Publications).

45. One helpful resource that provides the format, resources, and leadership notes to successfully accompany young parents in forming their children for first reconciliation and first communion is called *Growing Up Catholic.* It's available at ThePastoralCenter.com.

46. Monica wrote up her chat for this book a few days later. We have altered a few facts and changed some names to maintain confidentiality.

47. See *Growing Up Catholic Baptism Prep* by Paul Canavese and Ann Naffziger at ThePastoralCenter.com.

48. The resource offered by ThePastoralCenter.com includes seasonal letters, notes, and gifts for young families that will help them develop a Catholic flavor to their life. Regular accompaniment chats are also part of this. The resource is called *After the Plunge: Kit for Reaching Out to Parents After the Baptism.*

49. See *The Catholic Way for Confirmation* at ThePastoralCenter.com for a program that both offers deep insight into the content of the faith and provides formation in prayer.

50. Find *Sanctus* and other parish retreat resources in both English and Spanish at ThePastoralCenter.com.